Science meets Practice

Series Editor
Marko Sarstedt , Institut für Marketing
Ludwig-Maximilians-Universität München
München, Germany

Das Ziel der Reihe Science meets Practice ist es, den neuesten Stand der Forschung zu einem klar umrissenen Gebiet für Marketer aufzubereiten. Die Autoren vermitteln klare und auf den neuesten Forschungsergebnissen basierende Empfehlungen, die Marketer unmittelbar in ihrem Alltag einsetzen können. Um dieses Ziel zu erreichen, werden die Inhalte prägnant und möglichst anschaulich vermittelt, ohne jedoch an Stringenz einzubüßen. Videos und Zusatzinformationen auf Webseiten, welche über die Springer More Media-App abgerufen werden können, reichern die Inhalte an.

The book series "Science meets Practice" presents latest research on clearly defined topics for marketers. The authors provide concise recommendations based on the most recent research findings that marketers can immediately apply in their daily work. To achieve this goal, the content is conveyed succinctly and as vividly as possible, without compromising on rigor. Videos and additional information available on websites through the Springer More Media app supplement the content.

The series is bilingual, featuring works in both English and German.

Sascha Raithel • Setareh Heidari •
Jan von Schlieben-Troschke

Product Recall Management

Preparation, Execution and Recovery

Sascha Raithel
School of Business and Economics,
Marketing Department
Freie Universität Berlin
Berlin, Germany

Setareh Heidari
School of Business and Economics,
Marketing Department
Freie Universität Berlin
Berlin, Germany

Jan von Schlieben-Troschke
School of Business and Economics,
Marketing Department
Freie Universität Berlin
Berlin, Germany

ISSN 2730-714X ISSN 2730-7158 (electronic)
Science meets Practice
ISBN 978-3-658-45586-6 ISBN 978-3-658-45587-3 (eBook)
https://doi.org/10.1007/978-3-658-45587-3

Translation from the German language edition: "Produktrückrufmanagement" by Sascha Raithel et al., © Der/die Herausgeber bzw. der/die Autor(en), exklusiv lizenziert an Springer Fachmedien Wiesbaden GmbH, ein Teil von Springer Nature 2025. Published by Springer Fachmedien Wiesbaden. All Rights Reserved.

© The Editor(s) (if applicable) and The Author(s), under exclusive license to Springer Fachmedien Wiesbaden GmbH, part of Springer Nature 2024

This work is subject to copyright. All rights are solely and exclusively licensed by the Publisher, whether the whole or part of the material is concerned, specifically the rights of translation, reprinting, reuse of illustrations, recitation, broadcasting, reproduction on microfilms or in any other physical way, and transmission or information storage and retrieval, electronic adaptation, computer software, or by similar or dissimilar methodology now known or hereafter developed.

The use of general descriptive names, registered names, trademarks, service marks, etc. in this publication does not imply, even in the absence of a specific statement, that such names are exempt from the relevant protective laws and regulations and therefore free for general use.

The publisher, the authors and the editors are safe to assume that the advice and information in this book are believed to be true and accurate at the date of publication. Neither the publisher nor the authors or the editors give a warranty, expressed or implied, with respect to the material contained herein or for any errors or omissions that may have been made. The publisher remains neutral with regard to jurisdictional claims in published maps and institutional affiliations.

This Springer imprint is published by the registered company Springer Fachmedien Wiesbaden GmbH, part of Springer Nature.
The registered company address is: Abraham-Lincoln-Str. 46, 65189 Wiesbaden, Germany

If disposing of this product, please recycle the paper.

Preface

The book *Product Recall Management: Preparation, Execution and Recovery* delves into the complex realm of product recalls and the intricacies of managing them effectively. As authors, our aim has been to offer a comprehensive overview of this critical subject, carefully balancing research insights with practical applications throughout the book.

Our approach encompasses the latest research findings, complemented by a wealth of detailed case studies that illustrate key concepts and strategies. By doing so, we not only shed light on the significance of product recalls but also examine their multifaceted impacts on businesses from legal, non-financial, and financial perspectives.

Moreover, we explore the diverse roles played by various stakeholders, including customers, distributors, policymakers, regulators, suppliers, media outlets, investors, and financial analysts. Through an in-depth examination, we navigate through the entire product management cycle, delineating the pre-recall, recall, and post-recall phases.

Furthermore, we delve into industry-specific nuances, particularly focusing on variances between consumer goods, food products, and automotive sectors. By scrutinizing spillover effects and ripple impacts, we aim to provide a holistic understanding of the broader implications of product recalls.

In conclusion, the book culminates in summarizing the ten key insights gleaned from our exploration while also offering a forward-looking perspective on the future challenges and opportunities in the realm of recall management.

This comprehensive resource on product recall management is tailored to appeal to a diverse audience comprising managers and students but also educators and researchers grappling with the complexities of product recalls.

We express our sincere thanks to Shishi Liu, Senait Tenaw, Alexander Mafael, Stefan Hock, and Harald van Heerde for their support of this project. We also express special thanks to Eric Wagner and Marc Ruttloff from Gleiss Lutz as well as Chris Harvey and Matt Gigg from Sedgwick for their very insightful contributions to this book. Barbara Roscher, Birgit Borstelmann, Prashanth Mahagaonkar, and Ramya Prakash from Springer also provided invaluable and competent assistance in preparing this book. Finally, we thank the book series editor Marko Sarstedt for his support. We extend our heartfelt thanks to all of them.

Of course, the authors bear responsibility for any remaining deficiencies and errors.

Berlin, Germany

Sascha Raithel
Setareh Heidari
Jan von Schlieben-Troschke
June 2024

What to Discover in This *Science Meets Practice*

- This book serves as a comprehensive guide to product recall management.
- It summarizes and organizes the latest research in product recall management.
- It showcases all relevant aspects through more than 20 detailed real-world case studies.
- The book offers checklists and practical "how-to" guidance.
- It concludes with ten key takeaways every reader should know to master the challenges of product recall management.

Contents

1	**The Imperative of Product Recall Management**	1
	References	8
2	**Characteristics of Product Recalls**	11
	References	15
3	**Performance Implications of Product Recalls**	17
	3.1 Legal Liability Implications	21
	3.2 Non-financial Performance Implications	29
	3.3 Financial Performance Implications	34
	References	37
4	**The Roles of Different Stakeholder Groups**	43
	4.1 Customers	44
	4.2 Wholesalers and Retailers	50
	4.3 Public Policymakers and Regulators	53
	4.4 Suppliers	56
	4.5 Media	60
	4.6 Investors and Financial Analysts	63
	References	65

x   Contents

5   The Product Recall Management Cycle   69
    5.1   Pre-Recall Phase: Planning and Recall Readiness   76
        5.1.1   Cross-Departmental Product Recall Task Force   78
        5.1.2   General Product Recall Guidelines   81
        5.1.3   Training and Education Programs   82
        5.1.4   Mock Recall Exercises   83
        5.1.5   Product Tracing, Safety, and Quality Control   86
    5.2   Recall Phase: Process and Communication   87
        5.2.1   Problem Identification   89
        5.2.2   Risk Assessment   91
        5.2.3   Decision on Recall   91
        5.2.4   Recall Plan Creation   94
        5.2.5   Communication with Relevant Stakeholders   97
        5.2.6   Recall Execution and Monitoring   103
        5.2.7   Documentation and Reporting   104
    5.3   Post-Recall Phase: Recovery and Learning   105
        5.3.1   Performance Recovery   106
        5.3.2   Learning from the Crisis   108
    References   112

6   Industry Differences   117
    6.1   Consumer Products   118
    6.2   Food Industry   123
    6.3   Vehicle Industry   126
    References   131

7   Spillover Effect   135
    7.1   Spillover on Same-Company Products   136
    7.2   Spillover on Competitors   137
    7.3   Spillover on B2B Customers   141
    References   143

8	**Conclusion: Top10 Key Takeaways and Outlook on Future Challenges**	145
	Reference	151

Index 153

About the Authors

Sascha Raithel is Full Professor of Marketing at the School of Business and Economics, Freie Universität Berlin. Before earning his Ph.D. from Ludwig-Maximilians-Universität in Munich, he gained substantial experience as a consultant for various multinational firms. His research interests primarily focus on the impact of product harm crises on marketplace actors and the effective management of product recalls. Additionally, he explores market-based assets, particularly the creation, monetary evaluation, and vulnerability of assets such as reputation and brand equity. His expertise is frequently featured in leading TV and news media outlets, and he serves as a keynote speaker. His work has been published in renowned academic and practitioner journals, including *Management Science, Strategic Management Journal, Journal of Marketing Research*, and *Harvard Business Review*.

Setareh Heidari is a research associate and Ph.D. student in the Marketing Department at the School of Business and Economics, Freie Universität Berlin. Her research projects delve into the effective product recall management and its implications for firms and consumers. Before pursuing her Ph.D., she worked in the field of industrial engineering, bringing a diverse perspective to her academic journey.

Jan von Schlieben-Troschke is a research associate and Ph.D. candidate in the Marketing Department at the School of Business and Economics, Freie Universität Berlin. His academic pursuits center around consumer protection and the management of product recalls. At the heart of his research lies the notion of product recall effectiveness. In his research projects, he investigates the determinants of effective product recalls and their implications for consumers and firms. Prior to embarking on his Ph.D. journey at Freie Universität Berlin, he gained marketing experience through roles at Amazon and Coca-Cola.

1

The Imperative of Product Recall Management

Enter the realm of product recalls, where crises of massive proportions reverberate across industries worldwide. Picture the scene: In September 2016, Samsung's Galaxy Note 7 phones, touted as the pinnacle of technology, suddenly faced a mass recall of one million units (CPSC, 2016). The reason? Batteries overheating and exploding, leaving a trail of 26 burn cases and 55 property damage incidents in its wake. The costs for Samsung? $5.3 billion (Lopez, 2017).

Let us go back to 2008, when the Westland/Hallmark beef recall makes history as the largest ever. Over 143 million pounds of beef, once destined for dinner plates, now deemed unfit for consumption due to shoddy quality inspections (USDA, 2009). The fallout? Initial costs soared past $116 million, culminating in a $500 million settlement and the ultimate downfall of the company (Canavan, 2013).

Meanwhile, in the heart of the Chinese September 2008 milk crisis, the Sanlu infant formula recall unfolds like a tragic saga. Melamine contamination runs rampant, prompting the recall of 9000 tons of Sanlu's milk powder. The toll? A surge in kidney stones and renal failure among infants in China. Six lives were lost, 294,000 children were treated for illnesses linked to tainted milk, and the harrowing specter of bankruptcy looming over Sanlu. Facing significant debts from compensation claims, Sanlu declared bankruptcy in December 2008. Two men received a death sentence for selling melamine to the involved dairy firms (Wishnick, 2008).

But it is not just consumer electronics and food-facing product recalls. The automotive industry takes center stage, with, for example, Takata Corp's faulty airbags triggering in 2013 a recall frenzy of over 100 million vehicles sold by a variety of car brands. The outcome? A staggering $25 billion in costs, 27 confirmed deaths, and over 400 injuries—all from the expulsion of deadly metal fragments (Allianz, 2017; NHTSA, 2024; Klayman & Geoghegan, 2015). While Takata Corp filed for bankruptcy in 2017, millions of recalled vehicles including defective airbags remain on the road today (Hals, 2018; NHTSA, 2024).

And yet, these headline grabbing recalls are just the tip of the iceberg. Product recalls are a worldwide phenomenon. No sector is immune to the specter of product failure and recalls. Figure 1.1 illustrates that in the automotive, food, and consumer products sectors in the USA, EU + UK, and China, the number of annual product recalls was 10,954 in 2023. This figure has grown by 52% since 2013.

The surge in product recalls across various industries and regions can be attributed to multiple interconnected factors, affecting both the economic and the regulatory landscapes. Economic pressures prevalent in today's business environment often drive companies to implement cost-cutting measures, compromising product quality and safety. These measures may involve downsizing experienced staff and opting for cheaper suppliers, ultimately impacting the integrity of the final product. Additionally, the demand for shorter product development cycles to remain competitive further limits the time available for thorough testing and evaluation of product safety.

Moreover, the tightening of regulatory standards for product safety adds another layer of complexity. Companies are now required to meet increasingly stringent safety regulations, raising the risk of selling non-compliant products that may necessitate recalls. The Sanlu infant formula crisis serves as a stark reminder of the consequences of failing to adhere to regulatory standards (Wishnick, 2008).

Furthermore, the globalization of supply chains presents significant challenges in ensuring product safety. Managing and overseeing product

1 The Imperative of Product Recall Management

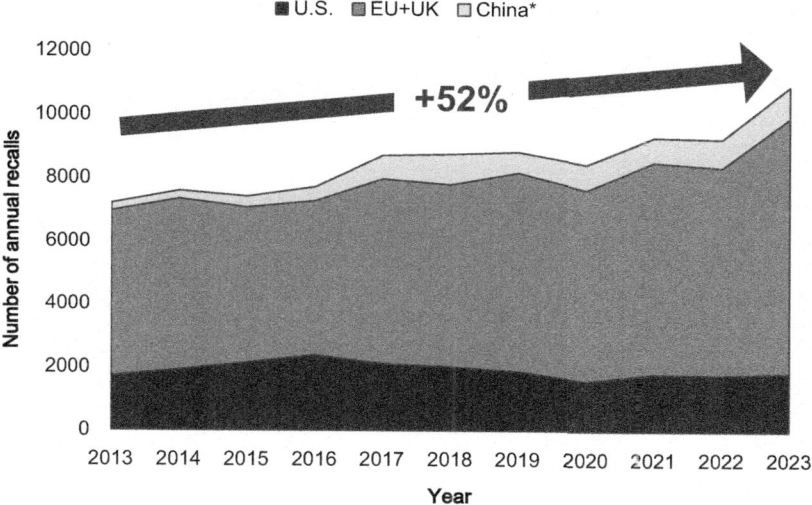

Fig. 1.1 Annual number of recalls in the USA, EU + UK, and China for automotive, food, and consumer products. * Food recall data for China not available. Source: Own illustration based on data from US NHTSA (https://www.nhtsa.gov/resources-related-investigations-and-recalls/annual-recall-reports), USDA (https://www.fsis.usda.gov/food-safety/recalls-public-health-alerts/annual-recall-summaries/summary-recall-and-pha-cases), US FSIS (https://datadashboard.fda.gov/ora/cd/recalls.htm), US CPSC (https://www.cpsc.gov/About-CPSC/Agency-Reports/Performance-and-Budget), EU Safety Gate (https://ec.europa.eu/safety-gate-alerts/screen/), EU RASFF (https://food.ec.europa.eu/safety/acr/reports-and-publications_en), and Chinese State Administration for Market Regulation (https://www.samr.gov.cn/zw/zfxxgk/fdzdgknr/zlfzs/art/2024/art_6a4d19d27bca422dbd726784d7439d0b.html)

safety become more difficult due to the complexities inherent in global supply chains. The testing of materials used in final products becomes more challenging as they traverse various suppliers and manufacturing facilities (Allianz, 2017).

Product harm crises and subsequent recalls have become pervasive in today's business landscape. Given the proliferation of expansive multinational corporations with intricate supply chains, coupled with stricter regulatory standards and heightened economic pressures, it is imperative to establish effective product recall mechanisms. These mechanisms are essential for limiting the harm caused by faulty and dangerous products to customers and the reputational damage suffered by recalling firms.

The following example boxes illustrate the stark differences between poorly managed and well-managed product recalls, emphasizing the importance of proactive recall strategies in safeguarding customer welfare and corporate integrity.

The Kinder Chocolate Recalls in 2022 and 2023

The Kinder chocolate recalls in 2022 and 2023 serve as a poignant reminder of the critical importance of swift action when product safety issues arise. In April 2022, Ferrero, a leading confectionery manufacturer, initiated a large-scale recall of several popular chocolate products under its Kinder brand. The catalyst for this action was a series of *Salmonella* outbreaks reported across Europe, directly linked to the consumption of Kinder chocolate (Verbraucherzentrale Hamburg, 2023).

By June 2022, the number of reported *Salmonella* infections associated with Ferrero's Kinder chocolate had soared to 324 cases, necessitating the disposal of over 3000 tons of chocolate products (The Brussels Times, 2022). Of particular concern was the fact that a significant majority of those affected were children aged 10 years or younger, underscoring the heightened vulnerability to severe complications, including dehydration, which can be life threatening, especially among the young and elderly (WHO, 2018). Investigation revealed that all contaminated products originated from a single factory in Arlon, Belgium, with Ferrero acknowledging the detection of *Salmonella* contamination in raw materials as early as December 2022 (PR Newswire, 2022).

Subsequently, Belgian authorities took decisive action by temporarily shuttering Ferrero's facility in Arlon and conducting raids on various company offices, seizing computers and documents. Ongoing investigations are focused on determining whether Ferrero violated its obligations as a food manufacturer and neglected to adhere to legal provisions concerning food safety and hygiene.

The financial ramifications of the recall were substantial, with insurance company Lockton estimating the costs to exceed $60 million (Lockton, 2022). However, quantifying the long-term revenue impact, driven by the erosion of consumer trust, proves challenging, particularly given the month-long gap between the initial contamination detection and the commencement of the recall.

Over a year later, in June 2023, Ferrero's Arlon production facility faced yet another shutdown due to another *Salmonella* contamination incident. This time, however, the company swiftly intervened to prevent contaminated products from reaching consumers, effectively mitigating potential health risks associated with their consumption (Verbraucherzentrale Hamburg, 2023).

Mattel's Toy Recall in 2007

In August 2007, global toy giant Mattel made headlines with a massive recall of millions of toys manufactured in China (Story & Barboza, 2007). The recall was prompted by the alarming discovery of lead in the paint of certain toys, posing grave health risks, particularly to children. Even minimal exposure to lead can have detrimental effects, while higher levels can inflict severe damage to the brain and nervous system, potentially leading to coma, convulsions, and, tragically, even death (WHO, 2023). Simultaneously, Mattel also recalled approximately 18 million toys containing magnets, identified as potentially hazardous due to their propensity to be ingested by children, resulting in serious health complications such as intestinal blockages necessitating surgical intervention.

Mattel's immediate response to these product issues is an example of effective product recall management. In stark contrast to the aforementioned example involving Ferrero in 2022, Mattel reacted swiftly to the discovery of the defects (just as Ferrero did in 2023), promptly initiating a widespread recall in collaboration with the U.S. Consumer Product Safety Commission (CPSC). The company adopted a proactive communication strategy, reaching out to 40 media outlets mere hours after the recall announcement. During the crisis, Mattel's CEO Bob Eckert personally shouldered the responsibility of engaging with external stakeholders, offering sincere apologies to affected customers, and pledging to bolster product quality and safety measures (Bartz, 2007; see Fig. 1.2). Eckert conducted 14 TV interviews and engaged in 20 calls with reporters in a single day, while the company fielded approximately 300 media inquiries in the USA alone.

The company also embarked on several advertising campaigns in leading publications such as the *Wall Street Journal*, the *New York Times*, and *USA Today*. These advertisements prominently featured a heartfelt, empathetic, and reassuring letter from the CEO directly aimed at the parents comprising the customer base (cited after Mcilroy, 2007):

> because your children are our children, too
>
> Dear Fellow Parents,
>
> Nothing is more important than the safety of our children. As a father of four, I share your focus on providing only what's best for them. As you may know, we've voluntarily recalled some toys for two different reasons: the impermissible use of lead paint and risks associated with small high-powered magnets.I want to be sure that every parent hears about these issues quickly, returns affected toys to us, and knows that we have already taken steps to further ensure the safety of our toys. Please visit mattel.com/safety / where you can learn about the affected toys, what we've done, and to find answers to your questions.
>
> Our long record of safety at Mattel is why we're one of the most trusted names with parents. And I am confident that the actions we are taking now will maintain that trust.
>
> You have my personal commitment that we are working extremely hard to address your concerns and continue creating safe, entertaining toys for you and your children.
>
> Sincerely,
> Bob Eckert
> Chairman & Chief Executive Officer
> Mattel, Inc.

Furthermore, Mattel took decisive steps to address the recalls by establishing a dedicated call center to field inquiries related to product safety issues, reaching out to millions of customers via phone or email to apprise them of the hazardous products. The company acknowledged its accountability in the matter and pledged to enact improvements.

In September 2007, Mattel unveiled a new three-point check system aimed at preventing future instances of lead contamination in toy paint (Deschene, 2007). Firstly, paint would solely be procured from certified suppliers, with each batch rigorously tested prior to purchase from the vendor. Secondly, the frequency of unannounced inspections throughout the production process was markedly increased. Lastly, every production run of finished toys would undergo comprehensive testing before being distributed to customers.

Moreover, Mattel exemplified its dedication to transparency regarding product safety and recalls by prominently featuring a "Recalls" link on its homepage, directing visitors to service.mattel.com/us/recall. This dedicated website serves as a comprehensive resource for current product recall information and facilitates consumer registration for immediate notification of any new recalls.

The financial impact of Mattel's toy recalls in 2007 was substantial, with estimated expenses totaling $40 million. Additionally, the company experienced a decline in revenue following the recalls, likely attributable to customer apprehension regarding the product defects (Forbes, 2007). However, had Mattel not responded as proactively and transparently as it did, the subsequent adverse effects of the recalls could have been even more severe.

1 The Imperative of Product Recall Management

Fig. 1.2 Mattel's CEO Bob Eckert's summary of the 2007 toy recall. Source: Snapshot from YouTube video (youtube.com/watch?v=9vuCd8Uzwek)

These two examples vividly underscore the pivotal importance of adeptly managing product recalls, revealing the stark contrast between mishandled and effectively managed recall processes. The repercussions of failing to address product failures can be profound for manufacturers, encompassing both financial and non-financial ramifications such as legal entanglements, erosion of customer trust, and in extreme cases, even bankruptcy.

In the forthcoming chapters, we embark on an exploration of product recalls and product-harm crises (Chap. 2), delving into the dynamics and implications of recalling firms' performance (Chap. 3). Subsequently, we shed light on the role played by various stakeholder groups in the realm of product recall management (Chap. 4).

Our journey continues as we furnish managers with comprehensive guidelines for navigating product recalls across the various stages of the process (Chap. 5). From crafting proactive recall strategies to adeptly communicating safety concerns to stakeholders and orchestrating post-recall recovery efforts, each facet is detailed, drawing from a variety of real-world case studies and cutting-edge research.

The consumer product, automotive, and food industries stand out as arenas particularly susceptible to frequent and high-impact product recalls. In acknowledgment of their unique challenges, we dedicate a special section to unraveling industry-specific nuances in recall management within these sectors (Chap. 6). Furthermore, we illuminate how spillover effects amplify the reverberations of recalls, often extending beyond the recalled products to impact the entire corporate portfolio and even reverberate across the industry landscape (Chap. 7).

Concluding our odyssey, we distill the essence of our insights into a compendium of Top10 recommendations, empowering managers to navigate product recall events with heightened efficacy (Chap. 8). The book culminates with a glimpse into the future challenges and developments poised to shape the landscape of product recall management in the years ahead.

References

Allianz. (2017, December 5). *Product recall risks growing in size and number as technology drives new triggers, warns Allianz.* Retrieved April 15, 2024, from https://www.allianz.com/en/press/news/business/insurance/171205-agcs-product-recall-risks-report.html.

Bartz, D. (2007, September 12). Mattel apologizes for recalls, backs stronger CPSC. Reuters. Retrieved February 8, 2024, from https://www.reuters.com/article/idUSN12248840/.

Canavan, N. (2013, March 28). The business of recalls: From Booming to Bankrupt. Food Quality and Safety. Retrieved April 15, 2024, from https://www.foodqualityandsafety.com/article/the-business-of-recalls-from-booming-to-bankrupt/.

Consumer Product Safety Commission. (2016). *Samsung Recalls galaxy note 7 smartphones due to serious fire and burn hazards.* Retrieved April 9, 2024, from https://www.cpsc.gov/Recalls/2016/Samsung-Recalls-Galaxy-Note7-Smartphones.

Deschene, L. (2007, August 20). *Five ways to do damage control like Mattel.* CBS News. Retrieved April 15, 2024, from https://www.cbsnews.com/news/five-ways-to-do-damage-control-like-mattel/.

Forbes. (2007, October 15). *Recalls cost Mattel in third-quarter*. Retrieved April 15, 2024, from https://www.forbes.com/2007/10/15/mattel-earnings-recall-markets-equity-cx_af_1015markets12.html.

Hals, T. (2018, February 17). Judge approves Takata's U.S. bankruptcy plan. Reuters. Retrieved April 15, 2024, from https://www.reuters.com/article/idUSKCN1G10SW/.

Klayman, B. & Geoghegan, I. (2015, May 20). *Timeline: Takata air bag recalls*. Reuters. Retrieved April 9, 2024, from https://www.reuters.com/article/us-autos-takata-takata-idUSKBN0O42QX20150520.

Lockton. (2022, May 12). A pricey salmonella case hits the product recall space. Retrieved April 15, 2024, from Lockton. https://global.lockton.com/gb/en/news-insights/a-pricey-salmonella-case-hits-the-product-recall-space.

Lopez, M. (2017, January 22). Samsung explains note 7 battery explosions, and turns crisis into opportunity. Forbes. Retrieved April 9, 2024, from https://www.forbes.com/sites/maribellopez/2017/01/22/samsung-reveals-cause-of-note-7-issue-turns-crisis-into-opportunity/?sh=7bb956a324f.

Mcilroy, M. (2007, August 14). Mattel hopes to reassure parents with print ads. AdAge. Retrieved April 19, 2024, from https://adage.com/article/news/mattel-hopes-reassure-parents-print-ads/119871.

National Highway Traffic Safety Administration. (2024). *Takata recall spotlight*. https://www.nhtsa.gov/vehicle-safety/takata-recall-spotlight. Accessed April 15, 2024.

PR Newswire. (2022, April 8). *Ferrero informiert über Rückruf ausgewählter Kinder-Chargen und Zusammenarbeit mit Behörden*. Retrieved April 15, 2024, from https://www.prnewswire.com/news-releases/ferrero-informiert-uber-ruckruf-ausgewahlter-kinder-chargen-und-zusammenarbeit-mit-behorden-850018447.html.

Story, L. & Barboza, D. (2007, August 15). Mattel recalls 19 million toys sent from China. *The New York Times*. Retrieved April 15, 2024, from https://www.nytimes.com/2007/08/15/business/worldbusiness/15imports.html.

The Brussels Times. (2022, May 19). *Up to 324 salmonella contaminations linked to Ferrero factory in Belgium*. Retrieved April 15, 2024, from https://www.brusselstimes.com/health/225970/up-to-324-salmonella-contaminations-linked-to-ferrero-factory-in-belgium.

U.S. Department of Agriculture. (2009). *Audit report: Food safety and inspection service oversight of the recall by Hallmark/Westland meat packaging company*. Retrieved April 15, 2024, from https://www.fsis.usda.gov/sites/default/files/media_file/2021-03/Audit_Report_Hallmark-Westland_Recall.pdf.

Verbraucherzentrale Hamburg. (2023, July 18). *Salmonellen: rund 300 Infizierte durch belastete Produkte von Ferrero*. Retrieved April 15, 2024, from https://www.vzhh.de/themen/lebensmittel-ernaehrung/schadstoffe-lebensmitteln/salmonellen-rund-300-infizierte-durch-belastete-produkte-von-ferrero.

Wishnick, E. (2008). Of milk and spacemen: The paradox of Chinese power in an era of risk. *Brown Journal of World Affairs, 15*, 209.

World Health Organization. (2018). *Salmonella (non-typhoidal)*. Retrieved April 15, 2024, from https://www.who.int/news-room/fact-sheets/detail/salmonella-(non-typhoidal).

World Health Organization. (2023). Road traffic injuries. Retrieved April 15, 2024, from https://www.who.int/news-room/fact-sheets/detail/road-traffic injuries#:~:text=Approximately%201.19%20million%20people%20die,adults%20aged%205%E2%80%9329%20years.

2

Characteristics of Product Recalls

> **What to Expect in This Chapter**
> - This brief chapter characterizes product recalls based on seven factors, including (1) legal weight, (2) safety violations and compliance issues, (3) initiation responsibilities, (4) recall management process, (5) motivations behind recall decisions, (6) voluntary and mandated recalls, and (7) recalls due to negligence and deliberate misconduct.
> - It differentiates types of product removals and related terms such as stock recovery, product withdrawal, (latent) product-harm crisis, product recalls as well as customer- and distribution-level recalls.

Product safety laws and regulations play a crucial role in ensuring the integrity of safety standards within goods. Nevertheless, the intricate nature of these laws, which exhibit variability across product categories and legal jurisdictions, can present obstacles in understanding the nuances of recalls and discerning them from similar events like product-harm crises. Astvansh et al. (2024) have pinpointed seven factors characterizing a product recall:

1. The concept of recall permeates both colloquial understanding and legal frameworks governing the safety standards within specific product categories. It holds a significant legal weight, potentially leading to civil or criminal repercussions. It is important to note that these regulations primarily pertain to tangible goods (rather than services) used by individual consumers or professionals.
2. A recall is warranted if it (a) possesses a defect posing a substantial risk to the user's safety and violates regulatory standards, (b) lacks a safety

flaw but fails to meet non-safety-related regulations, or (c) complies with regulations yet exhibits a safety flaw.
3. The responsibility for initiating a recall does not solely rest with the manufacturer; other entities along the value chain may also instigate recall proceedings.
4. The process of a recall involves a series of managerial decisions, with the initiation phase being the most conspicuous.
5. A firm's decision to initiate a recall can stem from various motives, including (a) demonstrating accountability towards customers, (b) mitigating potential product liability risks, or (c) a combination of both factors.
6. Notably, not all safety regulators possess the legal authority to mandate recalls. Among those empowered to do so, the preference often leans toward influencing rather than enforcing mandates. Consequently, a recall initiated by a firm could be either voluntary or involuntary, mandated by regulatory bodies.
7. While safety defects and non-compliance typically result from negligence on the part of suppliers and manufacturers, they can also arise from opportunistic behavior and deliberate misconduct (product tampering).

It is crucial to emphasize that not every instance of product removal from the market due to an issue constitutes a product recall. Figure 2.1 offers a comprehensive overview of the various reasons behind such removals.

Firms may choose to remove a product from circulation while it remains under their control, a process more aptly termed *stock recovery*. For example, it is possible that the product may fail quality assurance checks conducted by the manufacturer before it is distributed. What removal options are available if a product has already been distributed?

Even if the product poses no immediate harm to people, property, or the environment and remains compliant with regulations, there are valid reasons for its removal. These reasons may include market unsuccessfulness, inability to generate profit, end of product life cycle, insufficient quality, shortage of raw materials, patent dispute, and infringement of

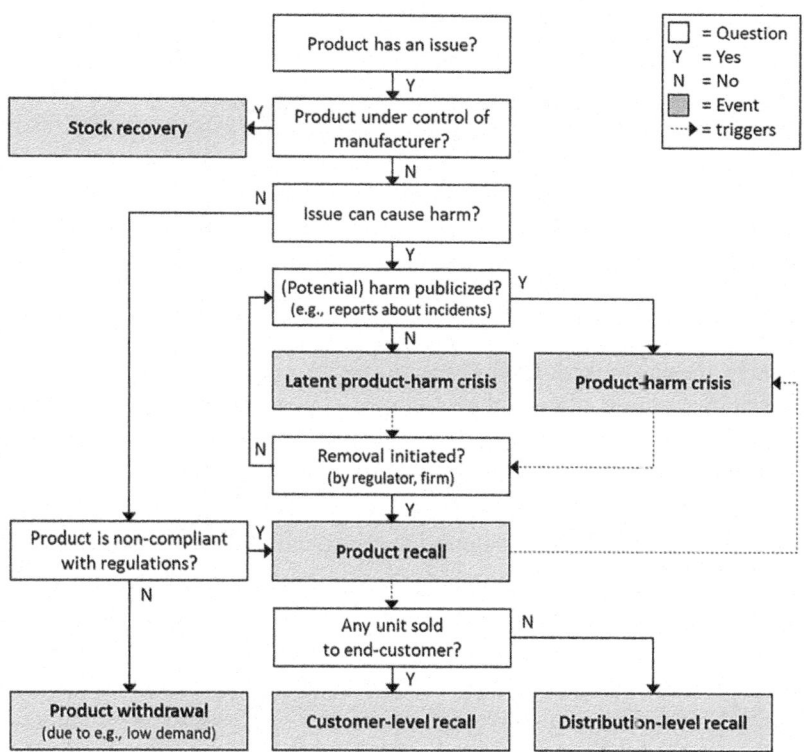

Fig. 2.1 Types of product removals. Source: Own illustration adapted from Astvansh et al. (2024)

property rights. This type of product removal is referred to as a *product withdrawal*. For instance, in response to damning product test results published by the German consumer organization Stiftung Warentest in 2024, retailers Edeka and Kaufland swiftly withdrew their private label olive oil products from shelves (Hertel, 2024). The testers raised concerns about the subpar quality of the products, noting their rancid or pungent taste.

However, if the product, while safe for use, is non-compliant with non-safety-related regulations, removal is still imperative, constituting a *product recall*. For instance, if a company fails to comply with labeling regulations related to ingredient disclosure or nutritional information on food products, regulatory authorities may mandate a recall to rectify the labeling discrepancies. While these issues might not directly pose safety concerns, they are nonetheless essential for consumer transparency and compliance with regulatory standards, thus warranting a recall to address this non-compliance (e.g., vegans would like to know whether a product includes animal produce or not).

In cases where the product poses potential harm (e.g., the product includes dangerous allergens that are not disclosed on the product label), a firm faces a *product-harm crisis* when the public becomes aware of the danger or, more commonly, when incidents causing harm to people or property are publicized. Even if the public remains unaware of the potential hazard, there is always the latent risk of it becoming public knowledge or an incident occurring. A *latent product-harm crisis* has the potential to escalate into an actual product-harm crisis once the hazards or incidents become public knowledge. At that point, firms face significantly more pressure to initiate a product recall. However, it's not always prudent to wait until then; instead, recalling the product before any harm or incident becomes public can be the wiser course of action (Raithel & Hock, 2021).

If safety concerns persist regardless of regulatory adherence and regardless of whether incidents have occurred, the company must make a decisive choice regarding the removal of the flawed product from the market and engage in cooperation with regulatory authorities. In instances of non-compliance with regulations, companies have little option but to engage in cooperation with regulators and initiate a product recall. When safety issues are not linked to regulatory violations, regulators prefer collaboration with the company. As already mentioned above, regulators strive to persuade companies to recall potentially harmful products at the earliest opportunity, yet they often refrain from mandating recalls due to the stringent legal prerequisites and the prolonged evaluation processes involved. If the decision to remove the product is made, it's termed a *product recall*.

Depending on whether the potentially harmful product has already been sold to and used by customers (consumers or professionals), the recall becomes a *customer-level recall*. If a product has not yet reached end customers and remains under the control of distribution partners, it falls under the category of a *distribution-level recall*. For instance, inspections may uncover instances where the cold chain was not properly maintained during transportation of a food product to the distribution partner and before the product was offered for sale. Alternatively, the distribution partner may conduct quality assurance checks and identify contaminations in the product. If such issues arise during this stage of the value chain, the partner notifies the manufacturer, initiating necessary actions.

Any product recall has the potential to trigger a product-harm crisis, even if the potential harm hasn't been publicized prior to the recall announcement because the recall announcement is typically made public through channels such as regulatory websites or press releases. Consequently, the public announcement of a product recall can raise concerns among customers regarding the safety and regulatory compliance of the company's products, thus potentially leading to a product-harm crisis.

The book delves into product-related issues that carry the potential to harm individuals, placing firms in the midst of product-harm crises and necessitating product recalls. Before we elaborate on the product recall management cycle, we delve next into the various ways in which product-harm crises and product recalls impact the performance of businesses.

References

Astvansh, V., Suri, A., & Damavandi, H. (2024). Brand warmth elicits feedback, not complaints. *Journal of the Academy of Marketing Science*, 1–23.

Hertel, M. (2024, April 18). *Nach verheerendem Olivenöl-Test: Edeka und Kaufland ziehen betroffene Produkte aus dem Verkehr*. Retrieved June 1, 2024, from https://www.merkur.de/verbraucher/kaufland-stiftung-warentest-duerre-klimawandel-schlechte-qualitaet-olivenoel-test-edeka-92909811.html.

Raithel, S., & Hock, S. J. (2021). The crisis-response match: An empirical investigation. *Strategic Management Journal, 42*(1), 170–184.

3

Performance Implications of Product Recalls

What to Expect in This Chapter
- This chapter explores the performance implications of product recalls, emphasizing legal, non-financial, and financial consequences.
- It discusses the financial burden of recalls, including direct costs like reimbursement and indirect costs like loss of trust.
- Legal implications are detailed, covering contractual, civil, regulatory, and criminal liabilities.
- Non-financial effects are examined, including their impact on customer satisfaction and brand perception, suggesting strategies for managing customer expectations and reputation during recalls.
- Financial performance implications are outlined, highlighting the potential negative impact on firm value, sales, and market shares, and offering insights into investor responses.

How the Ford Pinto Recall in 1978 Ignited a Debate over Profit vs. Safety
The Ford Pinto product recall in the USA stands as a notorious chapter in automotive history, largely due to the profound safety concerns surrounding the car's design. Introduced by Ford Motor Company in the 1970s, the Pinto, a subcompact car, quickly became embroiled in controversy due to a critical design flaw rendering it susceptible to fires in rear-end collisions. This flaw emanated from the placement of the fuel tank between the rear axle and the rear bumper, leaving it exposed to puncture upon impact. Consequently, collisions could rupture the fuel tank, leading to hazardous fuel leakage and the potential for fires or explosions (see Fig. 3.1).

The journalist Lee Strobel's coverage of the case, as documented in Strobel (1980), revealed that Ford was fully aware of this design flaw during the Pinto's development but chose not to implement modifications following a cost-benefit analysis. This analysis deemed it more economically viable to settle potential lawsuits resulting from accidents than to undertake a redesign of the car.

Despite Ford's calculated approach, a series of accidents ensued, resulting in injuries and fatalities, thrusting safety concerns into the public eye. Subsequently, in 1978, Ford initiated a massive recall of the Pinto, offering retrofitting options to equip the cars with additional safety features aimed at mitigating fire risks. While the company did not face criminal charges, it did become embroiled in numerous civil lawsuits related to accidents involving the Pinto.

One notable legal case was the state of Indiana vs. Ford Motor Company. In this case, the state of Indiana charged Ford with reckless homicide for the deaths of three teenage girls who died in a fiery crash involving a Ford Pinto. The prosecution alleged that Ford's decision not to reinforce Pinto's fuel tank, despite knowing the safety risks, constituted reckless behavior. However, Ford was acquitted of the charges in 1980. Additionally, Ford settled numerous civil lawsuits filed by individuals who were injured or lost family members in accidents involving the Pinto. These settlements were made to compensate victims and their families for damages resulting from the accidents.

The fallout from the Ford Pinto recall tarnished the company's reputation and eroded customer trust. The revelation that Ford knowingly marketed a defective product with inherent safety hazards undermined public confidence in the company's dedication to consumer safety. This erosion of trust serves as a stark reminder of the enduring repercussions stemming from the prioritization of short-term financial gains over ethical principles. The prioritization of profit over safety in this instance underscores the ethical quandary faced by corporations when balancing financial interests against public welfare. It prompts critical questions regarding the morality of weighing potential legal expenses against the tangible risks posed to customers. Moreover, the Pinto recall catalyzed heightened scrutiny of automotive safety standards and regulatory oversight. It underscored the imperative for stricter regulations to ensure that corporations prioritize consumer safety throughout product design and manufacturing processes, safeguarding against similar lapses in the future.

3 Performance Implications of Product Recalls

Fig. 3.1 Crash test video of Ford Pinto full-rear impact. Source: Snapshot from YouTube video (youtube.com/watch?v=IgOxWPGsJNY&t=104s)

The Ford Pinto recall stands as a poignant reminder of the ethical complexities inherent in product design and corporate decision-making, notably when safety is compromised for financial gain. Beyond its ethical implications, the recall underscores the broader impact of product failures and recalls, extending far beyond immediate financial repercussions. It sheds light on the potential enduring legal, non-financial, and financial consequences that can resonate long after the initial recall. However, our understanding of these consequences—be they legal, non-financial, or financial—remains an evolving area of research. We illuminate key findings in the following sections.

It is an unsurprising realization that every product recall constitutes a financial burden for companies. Direct costs arise from the recall, such as the reimbursement of purchase prices or repair expenses. Additionally, there are indirect costs because, for instance, customers can lose trust in the products of a manufacturer and may opt for a competitor's product in their next purchase decision. Furthermore, significant costs can arise from settlements with regulators as well as legal proceedings, especially when customers who have been harmed by a product demand

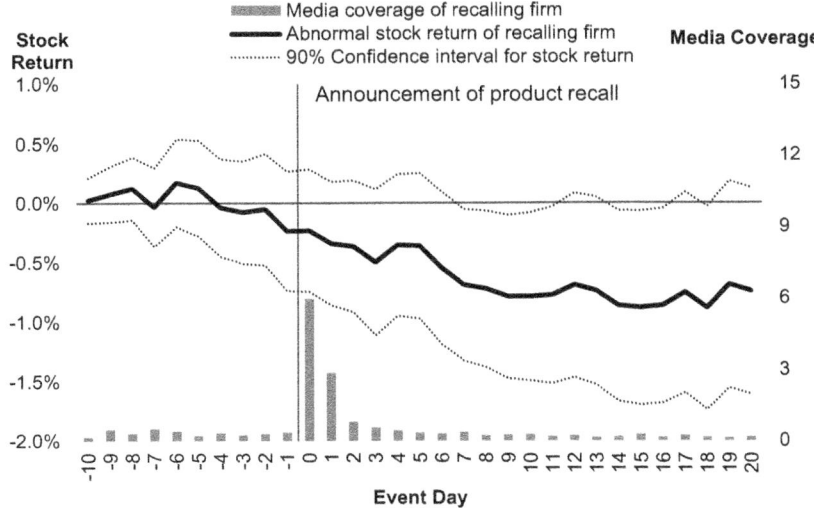

Fig. 3.2 Stock market losses of firms facing a product recall. Source: Own illustration, based on data from Raithel and Hock (2021), depicting N = 480 consumer product recall events in the USA between 1996 and 2014. The solid black line represents the average stock return (associated with left y-axis) of publicly listed firms around the recall announcement date, with stock returns adjusted by market return. The dotted black line depicts the 90% confidence interval, encompassing 90% of the observed events. The gray bars (associated with right y-axis) show the average number of Associated Press news articles covering product recalls of the focal firm. The x-axis displays event days, spanning from 10 days before to 20 days after the product recall announcement

compensation. One example is the bankruptcy of the Japanese company Takata, which occurred because it had to recall a massive number of airbags worldwide and faced severe legal ramifications (Soble, 2017).

Research findings indicate that, on average, product recalls hurt business performance and diminish the value of a company (e.g., Ameer & Othman, 2023; Chen et al., 2009; Hsu & Lawrence, 2016; Jarrell & Peltzman, 1985). The illustrative analysis in Fig. 3.2, examining nearly 500 cases of product recalls for consumer products (e.g., apparel, appliances, electronics, tools, and toys) in the USA, highlights that approximately 1% of market capitalization of publicly listed firms is lost on average. In 2023, the average market capitalization of an S&P 500 firm was around $30 billion. So, investors assume that the financial damage suffered by an S&P 500 company through one product recall is approximately $300 million.

However, research also emphasizes that the *range* of financial damages companies experience due to a product recall can be substantial, and a negative effect is not always inevitable (e.g., Liu et al., 2017; Raithel & Hock, 2021; Thirumalai & Sinha, 2011). The financial burdens for the company to rectify the product failure depend on various factors, such as the severity of the product defect, the number of recalled products, or the level of scrutiny in news and social media. But companies also have the opportunity to *manage* the effect of a product recall on their performance (Smith et al., 1996). A crucial performance metric in this regard is recall effectiveness (von Schlieben-Troschke & Raithel, 2024; Raithel et al., 2023), reflecting the company's ability to avoid incidents, quickly detect errors, achieve high customer participation in the recall, and promptly conclude the recall itself.

The following sections explicate how the nature of the product failure (hazard and recall volume) and the management of product recalls as well as recall effectiveness (incidents, detection speed, compliance rate, and compliance speed), influence future business performance (see Fig. 3.3). We analyze this business performance impact with regard to legal consequences from contractual, civil, regulatory, and criminal liability (Sect. 3.1), non-financial effects on customer satisfaction, brand perception, reputation, and trust (Sect. 3.2), and ultimately, the financial effects on sales, profits and firm value (Sect. 3.3).

3.1 Legal Liability Implications

A product recall can have significant legal liability consequences for the company involved. The specific implications of a product recall vary depending on factors such as the product's nature, the reason for the recall, managerial decisions made by the firm, and the jurisdiction involved. Possible legal liability consequences include:

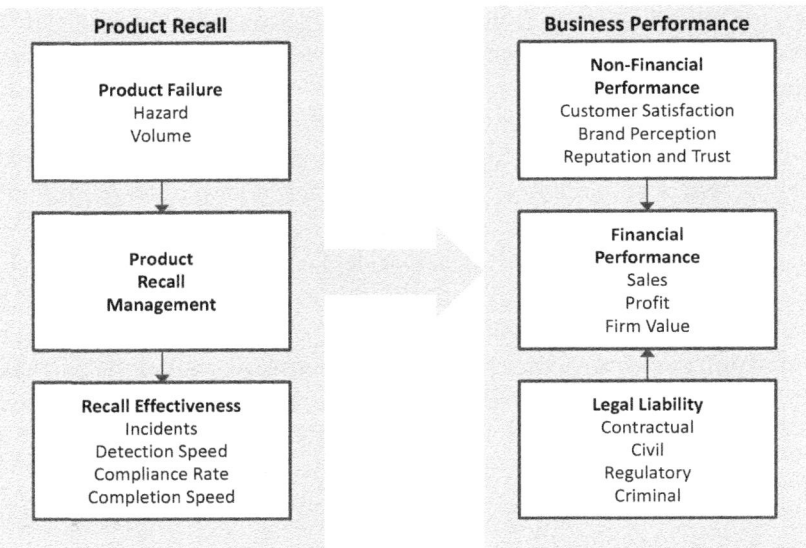

Fig. 3.3 Product recalls and business performance. Source: Own illustration

- *Contractual:* The contracts with suppliers, wholesalers, or retailers may trigger contractual obligations, including indemnification clauses.
- *Civil:* Companies may be held responsible for injuries, illnesses, or property damage caused by the defective product. Customers who have been harmed or incurred damages due to a defective product may file product liability lawsuits against the company.
- *Regulatory:* Regulatory agencies may conduct investigations to determine the cause of the issue and whether the company followed proper procedures. Failure to comply with applicable regulations and standards may lead to fines and penalties.
- *Criminal:* In severe cases involving intentional misconduct or negligence, individuals within the company may face criminal charges.

The following three cases highlight several aspects related to liability risks and legal consequences:

3 Performance Implications of Product Recalls

> **Boeing's Enduring Quality Issues**
>
> Industries like aviation are often subject to stringent regulations. A notable example is the aviation incident in January 2024 when a panel ripped off an Alaska Airlines Boeing 737 Max 9 during a flight, fortunately resulting in only a few minor injuries (Slider et al., 2024; see Fig. 3.4).
>
> The US Federal Aviation Administration, responsible for regulating such matters, promptly decided to ground most Boeing 737 Max 9 aircraft across all airlines under its jurisdiction until investigations concluded (Thorbecke, 2024). This immediate and rather drastic response of authorities is perhaps not surprising because Boeing had a history of safety concerns including two fatal crashes in 2021 (Isidore, 2021). Consequently, Boeing faced substantial financial consequences, including bearing a $21 billion burden. This encompassed compensation for affected airlines, costs related to delayed production and storing grounded jets, expenses from settling criminal charges, and the establishment of two victim compensation funds. The incident underscores the far-reaching legal and financial repercussions a product recall can have on a company.

Fig. 3.4 Alaska Air's Boeing 737 Max 9 loses fuselage section. Source: Snapshot from YouTube video (youtube.com/watch?v=uPzNKmbDAIg)

> **IKEA's Tip-over Issue**
> Legal liability risks for firms experiencing product failures and recalls can be substantial even in less regulated industries such as consumer products. A notable case involves IKEA, which had to compensate the parents of a 2-year-old child who tragically lost his life due to a dresser subject to a recall. The issue with IKEA dressers revolves around safety concerns related to tip-over accidents. IKEA dressers, particularly those from certain product lines such as the MALM series, were found to be unstable and prone to tipping over if not securely anchored to a wall. This instability posed a significant risk, especially in households with young children, as tip-over accidents could result in serious injuries or fatalities (see Fig. 3.5).
>
> In this instance, IKEA faced a financial obligation of $46 million. During the lawsuit, the parents asserted that they never received the recall alert issued by IKEA (Vigdor, 2020). The failure of IKEA's recall alert system may have influenced the parents' decision to pursue legal action against IKEA, highlighting the critical importance of effective communication and notification processes during product recalls.
>
> In response to this recall and the legal ramifications, IKEA implemented significant changes to its information policies regarding safety issues associated with its products. As of 2021, the company now mandates customers to complete a form, explicitly acknowledging the importance of following assembly instructions and anchoring furniture to the wall to prevent tip-overs (IKEA, 2024). This procedural shift not only reflects IKEA's proactive stance toward improving customer awareness and safety practices but also serves as a protective measure against potential future legal challenges in the event of tip-overs involving products purchased after this procedural change.

> **Volkswagen's Dieselgate**
> The magnitude of certain product recalls can lead to profound shifts in legal liability consequences. A prime example is the Volkswagen diesel emissions scandal exposed in 2015, involving the recall of a staggering 11 million cars globally, including 2.4 million cars in Germany. However, unlike their counterparts in the USA or Australia, German car owners initially lacked the ability to pursue collective compensation claims for the damages incurred.
>
> Recognizing the need for legal recourse, the German Parliament took decisive action in November 2018. To address this gap in consumer protection, they introduced a legal framework through the adoption of the "Musterfeststellungsklage," translating to Model Declaratory Proceedings. This landmark legislation enabled German consumers to collectively pursue

claims against corporations involved in fraudulent practices, setting a precedent for future cases. The Volkswagen scandal not only inflicted substantial financial repercussions on the company, amounting to a staggering €30 billion in fines, compensation, buybacks, and refits (Hessler, 2019), but it also left a lasting impact on the legal landscape in Germany. The introduction of the Model Declaratory Proceedings reflects a proactive response to ensure that consumers have a more accessible avenue for seeking compensation in the aftermath of deceptive product practices.

This legal evolution serves as a cautionary tale for companies engaging in fraudulent practices, as it has broad implications for potential legal ramifications arising from any future product recalls associated with deceptive or illicit activities. The Volkswagen case underscores the interconnectedness of financial penalties, legislative changes, and the evolving legal framework that can result from a high-profile product recall.

Fig. 3.5 Demonstration of the tip-over issue during a CPSC press conference in 2016. Source: Snapshot from YouTube video (youtube.com/watch?v=xEVybPp5VWo)

These three cases illustrate the significance of the behavior of companies before and during a product recall. Initiating a recall of defective products does not automatically absolve the manufacturer of their legal responsibility for distributing potentially hazardous items to customers (Crosley, 2020). Courts routinely assess whether not only fraudulent conduct led to a product recall, but also whether companies negligently delayed and could have withdrawn the product sooner. Similarly, during the recall, scrutiny extends to whether companies took comprehensive measures to inform consumers about the recalled products and continued to bear responsibility for preventing incidents caused by faulty products afterward. To establish this proof, it is beneficial for companies to align with the guidelines of the respective local authorities, which offer guidance on how to effectively structure a product recall. In this context, entities like the European Commission provide directives that assist companies in shaping effective recall procedures (European Commission, 2024). Comparable recommendations are also issued by other authorities, such as the U.S. Consumer Product Safety Commission (CPSC, 2024) or the Australian Competition & Consumer Commission (ACCC, 2024). In various countries, different authorities oversee distinct product categories, necessitating that businesses identify the respective regulatory bodies for each. Companies should then seek information from these authorities regarding regulations and directives pertaining to product safety and recalls. Implementing these recommendations from authorities not only safeguards customers from the consequences of product defects but also serves companies in mitigating potential legal repercussions following a product recall.

The following case study, provided by Gleiss Lutz—one of Germany's leading business law firms—examines a notable example of product safety issues and their potential legal implications.

Case Study: Faulty Gas Grill Kits and Manufacturer Liability
Prof. Dr. Eric Wagner, Lawyer, Partner, Gleiss Lutz[1] Dr. Marc Ruttloff, Lawyer, Partner, Gleiss Lutz[1]

Summary

In the realm of product liability and consumer safety, the case of the faulty gas grills presents a complex scenario that highlights the intricate balance between corporate responsibility, regulatory compliance, and the potential for civil and criminal liability. This case study examines the legal implications and the sequence of events that unfolded following the sale of defective gas grill kits by a well-established manufacturer.

Background

A series of incidents involving gas grills sold as DIY assembly kits in hardware stores have raised significant safety concerns. The grills, which required a special tool to ensure a gas-tight connection between the gas hose and the burner chamber, were distributed without this essential tool. Consequently, many consumers, lacking the proper equipment, resorted to manually connecting the gas hose to the burner chamber, leading to non-sealed connections.

Incidents and Damages

The improper assembly resulted in gas leakage along the sides of the burner chamber, causing side flames in over 20 reported cases. These incidents led to property damage, including scorched windows and house walls. Although no personal injuries were reported, the potential for such harm was evident, depending on the operator's proximity to the grill during ignition.

Corporate Response

Upon receiving complaints and damage reports, the manufacturer's quality management department, in collaboration with their insurance company, addressed the claims. As a remedial action, the company revised the instruction manual to include a safety notice emphasizing the necessity of the special tool for safe assembly. However, this updated manual was made available only online on the website of the manufacturer without any highlighting. No revised manuals were provided with the grills that were already in stock or in the process of being delivered.

Lack of Immediate Preventive Measures

Despite the severity of the issue, the manufacturer did not undertake other immediate preventive measures. For example, neither risk assessment

---

[1] Prof. Dr. Eric Wagner and Dr. Marc Ruttloff are both lawyers and partners at Gleiss Lutz, one of Germany's leading business law firms. They head the firm's Product Compliance Hub and have been advising domestic and international companies on product safety and liability for nearly 20 years. Together, they also host Germany's leading podcast on product compliance ("product.compliance.bites"), with new episodes released monthly.

> was conducted nor were any ad hoc measures such as a sales stop or recall notices for the products already in circulation implemented.
> *Escalation of the Situation*
> The situation escalated when a gas grill of the same model was used at a garden party hosted by a board member of the manufacturing company. The absence of the special tool led to another flare-up and subsequent property damage. This incident prompted the board member to alert the legal department, which then took swift action by involving external experts. The company then took all necessary actions, for example, conducted a risk assessment, imposed an immediate sales stop, and included the special tool and a revised manual with all undelivered products. Additionally, they issued a warning about the product hazards and informed the relevant authorities.
> *Legal Implications*
> The initial approach taken by the manufacturer was perilous. By acknowledging the problem and taking some measures, the company demonstrated awareness of the issue and the need for preventive action. However, the measures were insufficient to fulfill their product responsibility. This inaction exposed the company to significant liability risks and the individuals involved to the possibility of criminal liability.
> *Conclusion*
> The case of the faulty gas grills serves as a cautionary tale for manufacturers regarding the importance of proactive risk management and the potential consequences of inadequate responses to product safety issues. It underscores the need for comprehensive strategies to ensure consumer safety and compliance with legal obligations, thereby mitigating liability risks and upholding corporate integrity.
> *Reflection on Corporate Responsibility*
> This case illustrates that even professionally managed companies can underestimate such situations. The original handling of the incident by the manufacturer was fraught with danger, as it revealed a recognition of the problem and a perceived obligation to take preventive measures, yet failed to act sufficiently to meet product responsibilities. Such cases expose companies to high liability risks and individuals to the risk of criminal liability. It is imperative for companies to not only identify potential hazards but also to act decisively and responsibly to mitigate risks and protect consumers.

Beyond meeting regulatory requirements and acknowledging liability risks, managing the relationship with affected customers should be another major concern for managers. In the following section, we therefore analyze how customer satisfaction and brand reputation change in response to product recalls and remedial efforts by the company.

3.2 Non-financial Performance Implications

The impact of product failures and subsequent recalls on a company's overall performance has been extensively studied (Cleeren et al., 2013; Dawar & Pillutla, 2000). What is particularly intriguing is how product defects stack up against other corporate mishaps like communication breakdowns (Hansen et al., 2018). Surprisingly, only product failures, not other slip-ups, significantly tarnish a company's brand in the eyes of customers, both in the short and in the long run. This effect is so significant that severe product-related injuries can even sour the industry's customer satisfaction (Vaid & Donthu, 2023).

The root of this issue lies in the core function of businesses: selling products. Customers expect reliability and quality, and when these expectations are not met, disappointment sets in. In some cases, customers may even feel betrayed, turning their once-loyal brand love into lasting brand hate (Grégoire et al., 2009).

Research shows that the negative impact of product failures is heightened when the failure affects performance, poses a high threat to consumer health, and directly results in harmful incidents (Yang et al., 2022). However, how consumers perceive a product recall also depends on how well the company manages it. Customer satisfaction is not just influenced by the recall itself, but also by factors like the severity of the incident and the company's response, such as actions taken to rectify the faulty product (Mafael et al., 2022; Raithel et al., 2021).

Scholars often distinguish between partial and full remedies for product failures. Partial remedies might involve offering discounts or DIY repair kits, while full remedies entail replacing or refunding the product, or providing a full-service repair. The best approach for maintaining customer satisfaction hinges on the brand's perception prior to the recall and the severity of the product failure (see Fig. 3.6).

Companies facing an already tarnished reputation often find that a partial remedy suffices for minor product defects, given that customer expectations regarding quality and reliability are already low. However, there is an opportunity here for these companies to make a significant impact by demonstrating a strong commitment to enhancing product

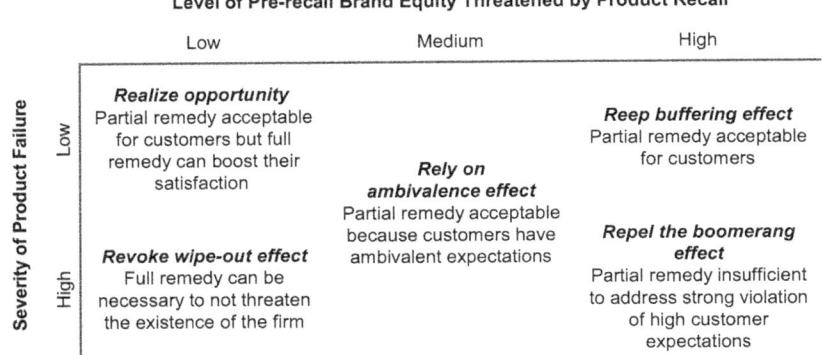

Fig. 3.6 Recommended actions to safeguard customer satisfaction after a product recall. Source: Own illustration based on Mafael et al. (2022)

quality sustainably. Offering a full remedy, even for minor issues, can help signal this commitment effectively (*opportunity effect* in Fig. 3.6).

When it comes to severe product defects, such as those posing a high risk to consumer health, providing a full remedy becomes imperative. Failure to do so risks permanently eroding customer trust (*wipe-out effect* in Fig. 3.6).

For companies with a moderate brand reputation prior to a recall, an *ambivalence effect* (see Fig. 3.6) may come into play. Consumers may not have strong opinions about the products, making a partial remedy economically viable to meet their needs.

However, for companies with a very high brand reputation pre-recall, the optimal strategy depends on the severity of the product defect. Minor defects may be adequately addressed with a partial remedy, leveraging the *buffering effect* (see Fig. 3.6). But in cases of severe defects, relying on this buffering effect can lead to a *boomerang effect* (see Fig. 3.6), amplifying customer disappointment due to sustained damage to product safety and quality. To prevent this, a strong signal, like offering a full remedy, is necessary to restore customer faith in the brand. The following case study on the Volkswagen Dieselgate (see also case description in Sect. 3.1) further illustrates this phenomenon:

> **Volkswagen's Dieselgate (Revisited)**
>
> The Volkswagen recall, involving millions of cars due to manipulated engine software, serves as a vivid illustration of the boomerang effect. Despite Volkswagen's strong brand values prior to the recall, the incident dealt a significant blow to its brand perception. Before the 2015 recall, Volkswagen held one of the highest brand values in the German car industry; however, the Dieselgate-triggered recall resulted in a remarkably sharp decline in brand perception, particularly within Germany. Interestingly, in the USA, Volkswagen's brand value was relatively low to begin with. The post-recall trajectory of overall brand value and customer satisfaction, as depicted in Fig. 3.7, presents a compelling narrative.
>
> A discernible drop in customer satisfaction is evident in both countries, with Germany experiencing a more pronounced decline, although this can be attributed to its significantly higher pre-recall satisfaction levels (not depicted in the figure). What is particularly intriguing is the subsequent recovery of satisfaction levels. Following a trough in the USA by the end of 2016, satisfaction rebounded. Conversely, in Germany, the decline persisted until the close of 2018. This begs the question: why the contrast?
>
> One significant factor is the variance in regulatory environments. In response to stringent U.S. regulations, Volkswagen adopted a more accommodating stance, implementing comprehensive measures to rectify issues and compensate customers (Howard, 2018; Bryan, 2016). Conversely, in Europe, Volkswagen pursued a less costly yet less effective strategy, adopting a defensive posture and requiring customers to individually seek compensation through an extensive and expensive legal process instead of proactively offering it. A pivotal moment occurred in November 2018 when the German Parliament took decisive action to bolster consumer protection. By adopting the "Musterfeststellungsklage," or Model Declaratory Proceedings., akin to the USA model, the Parliament introduced a legal framework that led to an uptick in satisfaction levels in Germany.
>
> These disparities highlight how distinct national legal frameworks and corresponding management decisions can yield differing effects on brand perception. It is plausible that Volkswagen could have expedited the restoration of customer satisfaction in Germany by emulating the strategy employed in the USA, despite not being mandated by German or European law at the time. Recent research on automotive recalls corroborates this notion, indicating that effective recall management safeguards customer satisfaction (von Schlieben-Troschke & Raithel, 2024), thereby yielding favorable financial outcomes for firms, as elucidated in Sect. 3.3.

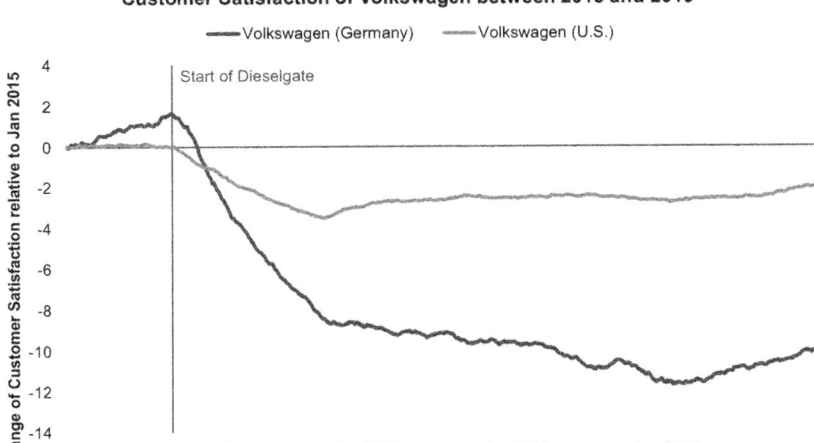

Fig. 3.7 Customer satisfaction of Volkswagen in Germany and the USA between 2015 and 2019. Source: Own illustration based on data provided by YouGov BrandIndex

It is vital to underscore that effective recall management, aimed at preserving customer satisfaction and safeguarding the company's reputation, does not always necessitate consistently opting for costly and intricate solutions. Surprisingly, research suggests that an overly cautious and excessively accommodating approach toward customers during recall management can backfire (Raithel & Hock, 2021). When a company fails to meet specific expectations in its recall management, termed *underconforming behavior*, it leads to more severe reputational damage compared to meeting those expectations through *conforming behavior* (refer to Fig. 3.8). A typical (or expected) response would involve offering an apology for the product failure and providing a straightforward solution to resolve the issue.

Strikingly, this research also uncovers that surpassing these customer expectations, known as *overconforming behavior*, can result in a disproportionately large reputational loss. This seemingly paradoxical phenomenon arises because customers may perceive such actions as an indication that the company is hiding something or that the issue is more severe

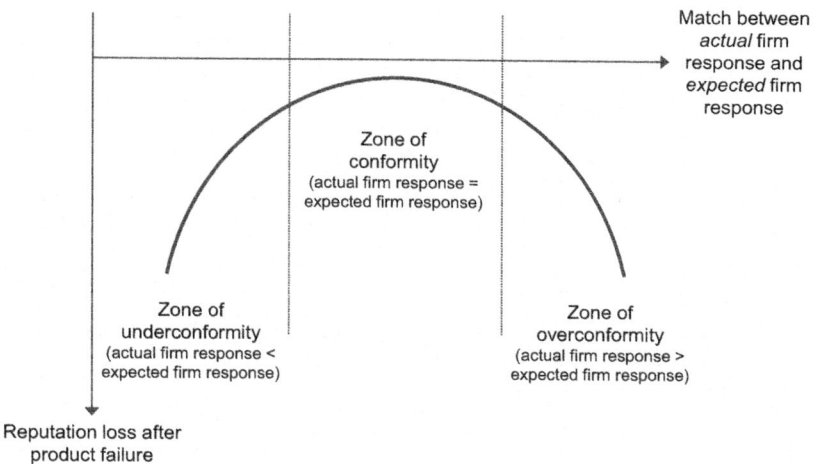

Fig. 3.8 Impact of conformity of firm response on reputation loss. Source: Own illustration based on Raithel and Hock (2021)

than portrayed. Otherwise, why would the company go beyond meeting their expectations?

Imagine this scenario: You are waiting on a train platform when suddenly, someone rushes past and accidentally bumps into you. Naturally, you are startled and perhaps a bit annoyed. Typically, the expected response would be for that person to apologize and explain the accident. Once reassured, you would likely move on from the incident without much fuss.

But what if, instead of just apologizing, that person offered you $100 for the inconvenience? At first glance, you might think it is your lucky day. However, upon further reflection, doubts may arise. You might question the person's motives and wonder if the accident was intentional. Similarly, when companies go above and beyond to address a product failure, it can trigger concerns among their customers.

Hence, the challenge in successful product recall management, while safeguarding customer satisfaction and reputation, lies in carefully aligning the measures taken with customer expectations. Interestingly, Raithel and Hock (2021) also demonstrate that investors anticipate these effects and respond similarly to consumers. We delve into the impact of product recalls and recall management on financial performance in the subsequent section.

3.3 Financial Performance Implications

As shown in Fig. 3.2 (at the start of Chap. 3), product recalls can significantly impact a company's value. However, this illustration does not fully convey the extent of these effects or the measures companies can take to mitigate these negative financial outcomes. In the worst-case scenario, recalls can lead to catastrophic consequences, as seen in the bankruptcies of companies like airbag manufacturer Takata, meat packaging firm Westland/Hallmark, and infant formula producer Sanlu (Wishnick, 2008; Canavan, 2013; Soble, 2017; also see Chap. 1). Even if bankruptcy is avoided, the financial fallout can be substantial, widespread, and long-lasting. Consider the case of Dutch medical device manufacturer Philips, which recalled 5.5 million respiratory devices in 2021. This recall had significant repercussions for Philips, resulting in a 70% decline in market capitalization, the dismissal of the CEO, and almost 13% of the workforce losing their jobs after reporting a net loss of 1.3 billion Euros in 2022 (Sterling & Meijer, 2022; Meijer, 2023).

These substantial financial losses aren't solely linked to the direct costs of recalls and expected legal expenses. Research suggests that investors often perceive the damage to a company as greater than the costs directly associated with the recall (Jarrell & Peltzman, 1985). This assessment stems from the spillover effects on the company's reputation and trust. Reputation damage can linger for a long time, jeopardizing the company's future market success (refer to the Volkswagen Dieselgate case study and Fig. 3.7 in Sect. 3.2). The extent of reputation damage and financial impacts depends on various factors. Several studies have explored the relationships between recall management, factors like recall volume, severity of failures, publicity, or competition intensity, and companies' financial performance (e.g., Borah & Tellis, 2016; Ferrer & Perrone, 2023; Hsu & Lawrence, 2016; Liu et al., 2017; Raithel & Hock, 2021).

The recall environment also plays a crucial role. Studies indicate that in recall clusters, where multiple firms receive faulty product parts from the same supplier, herding effects emerge. Early-recalling firms tend to face more significant repercussions from investors compared to those recalling later. The stock market penalty can be about 67% larger for firms that recall early compared to those that recall late in a cluster (Mukherjee et al., 2022). Similarly, in industries with frequent recalls, companies generally experience less impact from recalls compared to those operating in less recall-intensive sectors (Javadinia et al., 2023).

Investors tend to be risk averse and may initially overestimate the negative effects of a product recall. To counteract this potential negative overreaction, companies should provide investors with additional information about the recall. At the same time, companies should exercise caution in controlling their advertising expenses during and after a recall. Research suggests that advertising during a recall or when the recall is fresh in customers' minds should be avoided (Liu et al., 2017).

However, once the crisis is resolved, it is crucial to rebuild trust in the brand through a substantial increase in advertising spending to build trust in the brand. This is especially vital in competitive industries where customers have many alternatives available. While utilizing promotions to boost sales may seem appealing, research indicates that promotions are generally counterproductive (Liu et al., 2017). Companies should reintroduce promotions to the market only after genuinely overcoming the crisis.

As outlined in Sect. 3.2, understanding stakeholders' expectations for recall management is essential. Proactive recall management, involving timely voluntary initiation of a product recall, may trigger a negative investor reaction initially (Chen et al., 2009) but pays off in the long run (Liu et al., 2017). However, it is crucial not to exceed anticipated countermeasures excessively. Investors may become skeptical about the rationale behind such overconforming behavior, suspecting that the crisis is more severe than initially perceived (Raithel & Hock, 2021).

Another critical aspect of recall management is tracking the recall's success. Gathering information on how many products have been repaired, replaced, or disposed of is essential. Recall effectiveness directly impacts not only customer satisfaction but also the company's financial success, especially for high-volume recalls by a top-of-mind brand (Liu et al., 2017; von Schlieben-Troschke & Raithel, 2024).

In addition to analyzing the impact on firm value and investor response, it's crucial to consider the effect on customer behavior, such as sales and market shares. Effectively managing these impacts is vital because companies need financial resources to cushion immediate recall costs and legal expenses during product-harm crises. It is well-documented that product recalls initially have a negative influence on sales, and this effect can extend over a long or even indefinite period (e.g., Pennings et al., 2002; Rubel et al., 2011; van Heerde et al., 2007). However, research also indicates substantial variations in the size and duration of these sales effects, influenced by factors such as the severity of the crisis, media coverage, company responsibility, advertising decisions, and product prices (Borah & Tellis, 2016; Cleeren et al., 2013; Liu & Shankar, 2015).

> **Kraft Peanut Butter Recall in Australia**
>
> On June 20, 1996, the managing director of Kraft Australia received a troubling call from the local health authority: evidence of *Salmonella* had been found in their peanut butter. What followed became the most severe crisis in Kraft Australia's 70-year history, accumulating costs of approximately 15 million Australian dollars (Shoebridge, 1996; van Heerde et al., 2007). Subsequent investigations revealed that even more Kraft products were affected, leading to an expanded recall. By June 30, Kraft had to pull all peanut butter stocks from stores nationwide, impacting a staggering 70% of the entire peanut butter market in Australia. Within just 5 days, the company received around 100,000 inquiries from concerned customers and reported approximately 100 cases of *Salmonella* infections.
>
> Kraft faced criticism not only for the recall but also for its slow response to the crisis in the media. Additionally, the company was hit with a lawsuit from a law firm representing 540 customers. Distribution of all Kraft peanut butter brands was suspended for nearly 4 months. While it is no surprise that competitors capitalized on Kraft's absence from the market—Sanitarium, for instance, saw a 275% increase in revenue during the 4-month hiatus—Kraft managed to bounce back relatively quickly after the crisis. How did they pull it off?
>
> Firstly, Kraft stayed connected with its customers throughout the ordeal by establishing a hotline for direct feedback, which helped them tailor their recall and recovery strategy. Secondly, Kraft chose to prioritize its flagship brand, Kraft, over the also-affected brand, Eta (van Heerde et al., 2007). This meant that, post-sales stoppage, advertising efforts were concentrated on promoting the Kraft brand. Following the resolution of issues at the Melbourne factory, Kraft invested three million Australian dollars in national advertising to support the relaunch of the Kraft brand. Thirdly, Kraft benefitted from missteps made by its competitors, such as Sanitarium's decision to raise prices. Subsequent investigations suggested that reducing prices would have been strategically more advantageous for long-term market share gains against Kraft brands (van Heerde et al., 2007).

The Kraft peanut butter case highlights the significant impact managerial decisions can have on sales performance during and after a product recall. But can this case be applied broadly?

Research indicates that increased advertising spending can indeed influence customers to continue purchasing the brand (Cleeren et al., 2013). However, it is important to note that achieving the same sales effect may require disproportionately more investment in advertising (van Heerde et al., 2007; Liu & Shankar 2015). Moreover, the optimal advertising and pricing strategy depend on the amount of negative coverage the product recall receives and the extent to which the company is held responsible for the product failure (Cleeren et al., 2013). In cases of particularly negative coverage, it might make sense to significantly boost advertising spending.

However, timing is crucial here. Increasing advertising spending isn't necessarily advisable at the onset or peak of the crisis but should be implemented after overcoming it (Liu et al., 2017). When consumers attribute more blame to the company for the recall, lowering the product price could encourage purchases (Cleeren et al., 2013). Lastly, companies should be prepared for attacks from competitors seeking to capitalize on the product recall (van Heerde et al., 2007).

This chapter has illustrated that effective product recall management entails considering numerous factors and understanding the diverse effects on and feedback from various stakeholder groups, such as customers, investors, and policymakers. To provide further guidance, the following chapter will explore the roles of these different stakeholder groups before shining a spotlight on the product recall management cycle.

References

Ameer, R., & Othman, R. (2023). Stock market reactions to US Consumer Product Safety Commission enforcement actions. *Accounting & Finance, 63*, 3709–3735. https://doi.org/10.1111/acfi.13063

Australian Competition & Consumer Commission (2024). *Product safety responsibilities*. Retrieved April 15, 2024, from https://www.accc.gov.au/business/selling-products-and-services/product-safety-responsibilities.

Borah, A., & Tellis, G. J. (2016). Halo (spillover) effects in social media: Do product recalls of one brand hurt or help rival brands? *Journal of Marketing Research, 53*(2), 143–160.

Bryan, V. (2016, July 3). VW says U.S. 'Dieselgate' settlement not to be replicated in Europe. Reuters. Retrieved April 15, 2024, from https://www.reuters.com/article/us-volkswagen-emissions-ceo-idUSKCN0ZJ051/.

Canavan, N. (2013, March 28). The business of recalls: From Booming to Bankrupt. Food Quality and Safety. Retrieved April 15, 2024, from https://www.foodqualityandsafety.com/article/the-business-of-recalls-from-booming-to-bankrupt/.

Chen, Y., Ganesan, S., & Liu, Y. (2009). Does a firm's product-recall strategy affect its financial value?. An examination of strategic alternatives during product-harm crises. *Journal of Marketing, 73*(6), 214–226.

Cleeren, K., van Heerde, H. J., & Dekimpe, M. G. (2013). Rising from the ashes: How brands and categories can overcome product-harm crises. *Journal of Marketing, 77*(2), 58–77.

Consumer Product Safety Commission. (2024). *How to conduct a recall*. Retrieved April 15, 2024, from https://www.cpsc.gov/Business%2D%2DManufacturing/Recall-Guidance/How-to-Conduct-a-Recall.

Crosley, T.(2020, March 19). Who's liable when a recalled product causes an injury?. Crosley Law. Retrieved April 15, 2024, from https://crosleylaw.com/blog/dangerous-defects-whos-liable-when-a-recalled-product-causes-an-injury/.

Dawar, N., & Pillutla, M. M. (2000). Impact of product-harm crises on brand equity: The moderating role of consumer expectations. *Journal of Marketing Research, 37*(2), 215–226. https://doi.org/10.1509/jmkr.37.2.215.18729

European Commission. (2024). *Effective Recalls*. Retrieved April 15, 2024, from https://ec.europa.eu/safety-gate/#/screen/pages/effectiveRecalls.

Ferrer, R., & Perrone, H. (2023). Consumers' costly responses to product-harm crises. *Management Science, 69*(5), 2639–2671.

Grégoire, Y., Tripp, T. M., & Legoux, R. (2009). When customer love turns into lasting hate: The effects of relationship strength and time on customer revenge and avoidance. *Journal of Marketing, 73*(6), 18–32.

Hansen, N., Kupfer, A. K., & Hennig-Thurau, T. (2018). Brand crises in the digital age: The short-and long-term effects of social media firestorms on consumers and brands. *International Journal of Research in Marketing, 35*(4), 557–574.

Hessler, U. (2019, September 30). Class action lawsuit against VW in Germany. DW. Retrieved April 15, 2024, from https://www.dw.com/en/german-class-action-lawsuit-over-vw-emissions-begins/a-50596406.

Howard, E. (2018, March 29). VW's dieselgate fix for US cars is 'far more effective' than its European one. Unearthed. Retrieved April 15, 2024, from https://unearthed.greenpeace.org/2018/03/29/volkswagen-fix-us-europe-effective-dieselgate/.

Hsu, L., & Lawrence, B. (2016). The role of social media and brand equity during a product recall crisis: A shareholder value perspective. *International Journal of Research in Marketing, 33*(1), 59–77.

IKEA. (2024). *Safer homes acknowledgement*. Retrieved April 15, 2024, from https://www.ikea.com/us/en/customer-service/product-support/recalls/safer-homes-acknowledgement-pub59cfcaf0.

Isidore, C. (2021, March 10). The 737 max crisis costs continues to climb two years after the second fatal crash. CNN. Retrieved April 15, 2024, from https://edition.cnn.com/2021/03/10/investing/boeing-costs-737-max-crisis/index.html.

Jarrell, G., & Peltzman, S. (1985). The impact of product recalls on the wealth of sellers. *Journal of Political Economy, 93*(3), 512–536.

Javadinia, A., Gill, M., & Jayachandran, S. (2023). Recall environment and post-recall stock market response. *Journal of the Academy of Marketing Science*, 1–24.

Liu, Y., & Shankar, V. (2015). The dynamic impact of product-harm crises on brand preference and advertising effectiveness: An empirical analysis of the automobile industry. *Management Science, 61*(10), 2514–2535.

Liu, Y., Shankar, V., & Yun, W. (2017). Crisis management strategies and the long-term effects of product recalls on firm value. *Journal of Marketing, 81*(5), 30–48.

Mafael, A., Raithel, S., & Hock, S. J. (2022). Managing customer satisfaction after a product recall: The joint role of remedy, brand equity, and severity. *Journal of the Academy of Marketing Science, 50*(1), 174–194.

Meijer, B. H. (2023, January 30). Philips to cut 13% of jobs in safety and profitability drive. Reuters. Retrieved April 21, 2024, from https://www.reuters.com/markets/europe/philips-scraps-6000-jobs-drive-improve-profitability-2023-01-30/.

Mukherjee, U. K., Ball, G. P., Wowak, K. D., Natarajan, K. V., & Miller, J. W. (2022). Hiding in the herd: The product recall clustering phenomenon. *Manufacturing & Service Operations Management, 24*(1), 392–410.

Pennings, J. M., Wansink, B., & Meulenberg, M. T. (2002). A note on modeling consumer reactions to a crisis: The case of the mad cow disease. *International Journal of Research in Marketing, 19*(1), 91–100.

Raithel, S., & Hock, S. J. (2021). The crisis-response match: An empirical investigation. *Strategic Management Journal, 42*(1), 170–184.

Raithel, S., Hock, S. J., & Mafael, A. (2023). Product recall effectiveness and consumers' participation in corrective actions. *Journal of Academy of Marketing Science*, 1–20.

Raithel, S., Mafael, A., & Hock, S. J. (2021). The effects of brand equity and failure severity on remedy choice after a product recall. *Journal of Product & Brand Management, 30*(8), 1247–1261.

Rubel, O., Naik, P. A., & Srinivasan, S. (2011). Optimal advertising when envisioning a product-harm crisis. *Marketing Science, 30*(6), 1048–1065.

Shoebridge, N. (1996, September 2). Peanut butter king loses a kingdom Australian Financial Review. Retrieved April 15, 2024, from https://www.afr.com/companies/peanut-butter-king-loses-a-kingdom-19960902-kaymq.

Slider, A., Maidenberg, M. & Tangel, A. (2024, January 9). Alaska airlines Boeing probe: What we know. *The Wall Street Journal*. Retrieved April 15, 2024, from https://www.wsj.com/business/airlines/alaska-airlines-boeing-737-max-9-probe-d1af9026.

Smith, N. C., Thomas, R. J., & Quelch, J. (1996). A strategic approach to managing product recalls. *Harvard Business Review*. Retrieved February 8, 2024, from https://hbr.org/1996/09/a-strategic-approach-to-managing-product-recalls.

Soble, J. (2017, June 25). Takata, unable to overcome airbag crisis, files for bankruptcy protection. *The New York Times*. Retrieved April 19, 2024, from https://www.nytimes.com/2017/06/25/business/takata-japan-restructuring.html.

Sterling, T. & Meijer, B. H. (2022, October 24). Philips to cut 5% of workforce as new CEO acts to counter falling sales. Reuters. Retrieved April 21, 2024, from https://www.reuters.com/business/philips-cut-4000-jobs-after-medical-equipment-recall-2022-10-24/.

Strobel, L. P. (1980). *Reckless homicide?: Ford's pinto trial*. And Books.

Thirumalai, S., & Sinha, K. K. (2011). Product recalls in the medical device industry: An empirical exploration of the sources and financial consequences. *Management Science, 57*(2), 376–392.

Thorbecke, C. (2024, January 10). Boeing CEO acknowledges 'mistake' related to terrifying Alaska Airlines flight. CNN. Retrieved April 15, 2024, from https://edition.cnn.com/2024/01/09/business/boeing-safety-meeting-737-max-factory/index.html.

Vaid, S., & Donthu, N. (2023). When injured product users may also stay satisfied: A macro-level analysis. *Journal of Business Research, 162*, 113887.

Van Heerde, H., Helsen, K., & Dekimpe, M. G. (2007). The impact of a product-harm crisis on marketing effectiveness. *Marketing Science, 26*(2), 230–245.

Vigdor, N. (2020, June 1). Ikea will pay $46 million to parents of toddler crushed to death by a dresser. *The New York Times*. Retrieved April 15, 2024, from https://www.nytimes.com/2020/01/06/us/ikea-dresser-lawsuit-settlement.html.

von Schlieben-Troschke, J., & Raithel, S. (2024). The financial performance impact of product recall compliance. Proceedings of the European Marketing Academy, 53rd.

Wishnick, E. (2008). Of milk and spacemen: The paradox of Chinese power in an era of risk. *Brown Journal of World Affairs, 15*, 209.

Yang, Z., Freling, T., Sun, S., & Richardson-Greenfield, P. (2022). When do product crises hurt business? A meta-analytic investigation of negative publicity on consumer responses. *Journal of Business Research, 150*, 102–120.

4

The Roles of Different Stakeholder Groups

> **What to Expect in This Chapter**
> - This chapter explores the roles of different stakeholder groups including customers, wholesalers and retailers, policymakers and regulators, suppliers, media as well as investors and financial analysts.
> - It highlights the significance of addressing each stakeholder group's needs and showing transparent management practices in maintaining stakeholder trust and market standing.
> - It explains how each stakeholder group contributes to the success of the recall process.
> - It outlines potential challenges in product recall management, including low consumer awareness, communication breakdowns with retailers, and resistance to engaging with the media.
> - It discusses collaborative solutions involving all stakeholders to address these challenges effectively.

In handling product recalls, it is essential to embrace a customer-focused mindset to uphold positive relationships throughout the ordeal (*customer-centric perspective*). This involves not just addressing the concerns of end users but also collaborating with distributors like wholesalers and retailers. Moreover, it is crucial to recognize the significance of various stakeholders such as public policymakers, regulators, suppliers, the media, investors, and financial analysts (Li et al., 2022).

These stakeholders play a pivotal role in the recall process, each with their own set of information needs. Engaging them can garner crucial support and enhance the firm's ability to manage the recall effectively.

Furthermore, these stakeholders wield influence over customer perceptions during and after the recall, thereby impacting the company's overall performance in the short and long term.

By prioritizing a customer-centric strategy and taking into account the perspectives of all stakeholders involved, product recall management can adeptly navigate challenges while safeguarding trust and minimizing disruptions to relationships with customers and other vital parties. In the subsequent sections, we delve deeply into each stakeholder group, exploring their unique needs, inquiries, and significant challenges that must be addressed effectively.

4.1 Customers

During a product recall, customers are pivotal in safeguarding both their safety and the efficacy of the recall procedure. Initially, customers need to stay abreast of any recall alerts issued by manufacturers, retailers, or regulatory agencies. Upon receiving such notifications, it is imperative for customers to check if they possess the affected product.

Should customers discover they have the recalled item, prompt cessation of its use is frequently essential to prevent potential harm or further damage. Subsequently, customers are typically advised to return the product to the manufacturer, retailer, or a designated location for appropriate disposal, repair, or replacement. Adhering to the instructions outlined in the recall notice is crucial for ensuring a seamless and efficient recall process.

Moreover, customers are encouraged to provide feedback to the manufacturer or regulatory bodies regarding their encounter with the recalled product. This feedback aids in enhancing future product safety measures and refining recall protocols, thereby enhancing consumer protection in subsequent incidents. Additionally, customers can assist in disseminating awareness of the recall within their social circles, ensuring that more affected individuals are promptly informed and able to take necessary actions.

Throughout a product recall, various challenges may arise, impacting both the efficiency of the recall process and customer safety. These

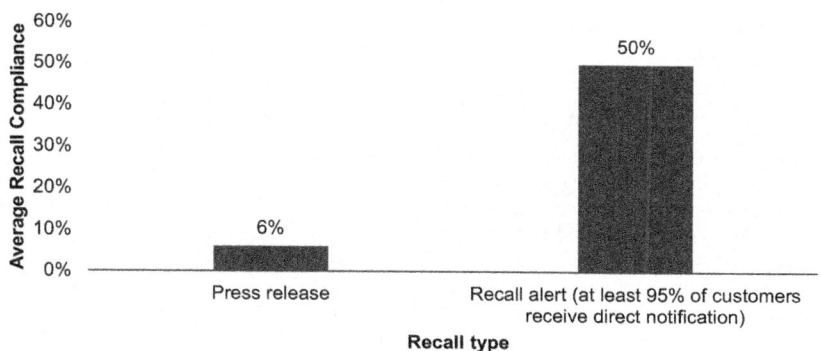

Fig. 4.1 Average recall compliance by communication channel. Source: Illustration rebuilt with data from Cave (2017)

challenges include low customer awareness, underscoring the need for comprehensive customer notification to prevent continued use of the recalled product. One of the biggest challenges is reaching out to and creating awareness for the recall among affected customers. One of the most significant hurdles involves raising awareness of the recall among affected customers. A *recall alert* (the company is able to contact at least 95% of affected customers through direct communication) substantially boosts average participation in consumer product recalls compared to press releases, increasing it from approximately 6%–50% (Cave, 2017; see also Fig. 4.1).

Additionally, difficulties in identifying affected items and limited options for their return or replacement can hinder customers' ability to address the issue effectively. Inconsistent execution of the recall process by retailers across different regions may lead to confusion, while disruptions in the supply chain can cause delays in retrieving and replacing the recalled products. Furthermore, perceived mismanagement or lack of accountability from manufacturers or regulatory bodies may exacerbate customer distrust and resentment. Addressing these challenges requires collaborative efforts among all stakeholders to ensure clear communication, prompt action, and protection of customer well-being throughout the recall process. The following example highlights some of these challenges.

> **The General Motors Faulty Ignition Switch Recall**
> In 2014, General Motors (GM) faced a major product recall due to a faulty ignition switch in 2.6 million vehicles. The defect could cause the engine to shut off unexpectedly, disabling critical safety features like airbags. As of 2015, 97 deaths are linked to this malfunction (Plumer, 2015). Customers distrusted GM due to its delayed response and perceived lack of transparency. The company had known about the issue for years before taking action, fueling worries about prioritizing cost-cutting over safety, leading to confusion and skepticism.
>
> GM's communication about the recall was also criticized for being unclear, exacerbating customer mistrust. Some customers hesitated to respond to the recall notices or ignored the warnings because the recall notification was not serious enough (CBS, 2014), hindering the effectiveness of the recall process and prolonging the safety risks associated with the faulty ignition switch. Figure 4.2 shows the criticized owner notification letter.
>
> Then, customers were frustrated by facing weeks and months before the car could be fixed at a dealer (Krisher, 2014). Finally, some customers felt GM's compensation offers for accidents or injuries caused by the defect were inadequate. The GM ignition switch recall serves as a reminder of the importance of transparent and clear communication, prompt action, and fair compensation in earning and maintaining customer trust during product recalls.

In summary, creating active engagement and cooperation of customers are indispensable for the successful execution of a product recall. Through prompt response to recall notifications, cessation of the use of affected products, adherence to return or disposal instructions, provision of feedback, and dissemination of awareness, customers significantly contribute to upholding consumer safety and ensuring the integrity of the recall process. In Chap. 5 (Product Recall Management Cycle), we will explore how these challenges can be addressed, and the recall process can be managed successfully.

Representative Letter – Customer letters are brand, model and model year specific; listing the 17-digit VIN and are personalized.

IMPORTANT SAFETY RECALL

April 2014

Dear GM Customer:

This notice is sent to you in accordance with the National Traffic and Motor Vehicle Safety Act.

General Motors has decided that one or more defects as described below which relate to motor vehicle safety may exist in all 2008-2010 model year (MY) Chevrolet Cobalt, 2008-2011 MY Chevrolet HHR, 2008-2010 MY Pontiac Solstice, 2008-2010 MY Pontiac G5, and 2008-2010 MY Saturn Sky vehicles. As a result, GM is conducting a recall. We apologize for this inconvenience. However, we are concerned about your safety and continued satisfaction with our products.

IMPORTANT

- This notice applies to your 2008-2010 MY Chevrolet Cobalt, 2008-2011 MY Chevrolet HHR, 2008-2010 MY Pontiac Solstice, 2008-2010 MY Pontiac G5, and 2008-2010 MY Saturn Sky, VIN _____.

  Until the recall repairs have been performed, it is <u>very</u> important that you remove all items from your key ring, leaving only the vehicle key. The key fob (if applicable), should also be removed from your key ring. Also, when exiting your vehicle, always make sure your vehicle is in "Park", or in the case of a manual transmission, put the transmission into reverse gear and set the parking brake.

- Parts are not presently available to remedy your vehicle. When parts become available, GM will send you another letter to notify you to schedule an appointment with your GM dealer.

- The recall will be performed for you at **no charge**.

Why is your vehicle being recalled?	GM records indicate a defective Ignition & Start Switch or a kit containing a defective Ignition & Start Switch may have been installed in some 2008-2010 MY Chevrolet Cobalt, 2008-2011 MY Chevrolet HHR, 2008-2010 MY Pontiac Solstice, 2008-2010 MY Pontiac G5, and 2008-2010 MY Saturn Sky vehicles.
	If your vehicle has the defective Ignition & Start Switch, there is a risk, under certain conditions, that your ignition switch may move out of the "run" position, resulting in a partial loss of electrical power and turning

Fig. 4.2 GM's faulty ignition switch recall: Owner notification letter. Source: NHTSA (2014)

off the engine. This risk increases if your key ring is carrying added weight (such as more keys or the key fob) or your vehicle experiences rough road conditions or other jarring or impact related events. If the ignition switch is not in the run position, the air bags may not deploy if the vehicle is involved in a crash, increasing the risk of injury or fatality.

Some of these vehicles may also have a condition in which the ignition key may be removed when the ignition is not in the "Off" position. If the ignition key is removed when the ignition is not in the "Off" position, unintended vehicle motion may occur: (a) for an automatic transmission, if the transmission is not in "Park"; or (b) for a manual transmission, if the parking brake is not engaged and the transmission is not in reverse gear. This could result in a vehicle crash and occupant or pedestrian injuries.

Until the recall repairs have been performed, it is _very_ important that you remove all items from your key ring, leaving only the vehicle key. The key fob (if applicable), should also be removed from your key ring. Also, when exiting your vehicle, always make sure your vehicle is in "Park", or in the case of a manual transmission, put the transmission into reverse gear and set the parking brake.

What will we do?	Whether or not your ignition switch has been previously serviced, GM will replace the ignition switch on your vehicle. This measure is being taken in an abundance of caution, to make sure all defective ignition switches have been removed from all vehicles.

PARTS ARE NOT CURRENTLY AVAILABLE, but when parts are available, your GM dealer will replace the ignition switch on your vehicle whether it is the original switch or a replacement, and for vehicles that have not previously had an ignition cylinder replacement under warranty, dealers will replace the ignition cylinder. Dealers will also cut and if necessary re-learn two ignition keys for each vehicle. This service will be performed for you at **no charge**. Because of scheduling requirements, it is likely that your dealer will need your vehicle longer than the actual service correction time of approximately 90 minutes.

We are working as quickly as possible to obtain parts. We will notify you with at least a second letter as soon as parts are available so that you can schedule an appointment with your dealer to have your vehicle repaired.

If required, your GM dealer will provide you with some form of courtesy transportation at no charge while your vehicle is at the dealership for this repair. |
| What should you do? | When GM notifies you that parts are available, you should contact your GM dealer to arrange a service appointment. **Until the recall repairs have been performed, it is _very_ important that you** |

Fig. 4.2 (continued)

4 The Roles of Different Stakeholder Groups

remove all items from your key ring, leaving only the vehicle key. The key fob (if applicable), should also be removed from your key ring. Also, when exiting your vehicle, always make sure your vehicle is in "Park", or in the case of a manual transmission, put the transmission into reverse gear and set the parking brake.

Did you already pay for this repair? When GM notifies you that parts are available, GM will also provide instructions for you to request reimbursement if you paid for repairs for the recall condition previously.

Do you have questions? If you have questions or concerns that your dealer is unable to resolve, please contact the appropriate Customer Assistance Center at the number listed below.

Division	Number	Text Telephones (TTY)
Chevrolet	1-800-222-1020	1-800-833-2438
Pontiac	1-800-762-2737	1-800-833-7668
Saturn	1-800-553-6000	1-800-833-6000
Puerto Rico – English	1-800-496-9992	
Puerto Rico – Español	1-800-496-9993	
Virgin Islands	1-800-496-9994	

If after contacting your dealer and the Customer Assistance Center, you are still not satisfied we have done our best to remedy this condition without charge and within a reasonable time, you may wish to write the Administrator, National Highway Traffic Safety Administration, 1200 New Jersey Avenue, SE., Washington, DC 20590, or call the toll-free Vehicle Safety Hotline at 1.888.327.4236 (TTY 1.800.424.9153), or go to http://www.safercar.gov. The National Highway Traffic Safety Administration Campaign ID Numbers for these recalls are 14V047 and 14V171.

Federal regulation requires that any vehicle lessor receiving this recall notice must forward a copy of this notice to the lessee within ten days.

For additional information regarding this recall, please go to www.gmignitionupdate.com.

General Director,
Customer and Relationship Services

GM Recall Numbers: 14092 and 14113 or 14133

Fig. 4.2 (continued)

4.2 Wholesalers and Retailers

Wholesalers and retailers play vital roles when a product recall occurs, acting as the main points of contact for customers encountering issues with a product. For manufacturers, receiving timely notifications from these distributors about potential problems is crucial for detecting product issues early on.

During a product recall, it is essential for manufacturers to work closely with distributors to pinpoint and isolate affected products in their inventory, putting a stop to further distribution. Manufacturers should also assist distributors in swiftly retrieving impacted products from end customers or retailers. This collaborative effort is pivotal, especially as distributors may need to work with regulatory authorities to provide necessary information and assistance throughout the recall process.

Moreover, distributors are responsible for informing customers about the recall and guiding them on how to return or dispose of affected items. Retailers often oversee the return and refund procedures to ensure affected customers are appropriately compensated. Keeping detailed records of recalled products, including quantities, dates, and destinations, is crucial for distributors and instrumental for manufacturers to track recalled products and ensure regulatory compliance.

Therefore, it is important for manufacturers to establish strong communication channels with wholesalers and retailers to facilitate timely notification and coordination during recall events. Providing comprehensive training and support materials to these partners helps clarify their roles and responsibilities, ensuring adherence to recall protocols. Additionally, maintaining visibility throughout the supply chain enables prompt identification of affected products and communication of recall information to downstream partners. Allocating resources to support wholesalers and retailers, whether through logistical assistance or financial aid for refunds, is often necessary to ensure the recall is executed effectively.

> **The Samsung Galaxy Note 7 Recall**
>
> The Samsung Galaxy Note 7 recall of 2016 stands out as a landmark event in the history of consumer electronics, marked by reports of devices catching fire or exploding, linked to a battery defect. In response, Samsung took decisive action by launching a worldwide recall and suspending sales of the smartphone.
>
> What makes this recall distinctive is Samsung's direct outreach to owners through safety messages displayed on the device screen (see Fig. 4.3). Additionally, Samsung devoted significant resources to streamlining the return process, providing detailed return instructions (see Fig. 4.3).
>
> However, the recall process encountered significant hurdles, particularly regarding the involvement of retailers and their interaction with customers (Selyukh, 2016). Many retailers found themselves unprepared to manage the recall, lacking clear guidance or protocols from Samsung. Consequently, some continued to sell the potentially unsafe devices even after the recall announcement, leading to confusion and frustration among consumers.
>
> Customers encountered difficulties when attempting to return or exchange their devices at retailers, facing inconsistent policies and lengthy delays in refund processing. One notable challenge was the complex procedure for returning a phone to a retailer and seamlessly transferring data and settings to a replacement device. Adding to the complication, certain retailers prohibited customers from turning on their phones within the store, hampering the smooth transfer of data to the new device (Anwyl, 2016).
>
> This ineffective communication and coordination between Samsung and retailers worsened these challenges, resulting in widespread dissatisfaction and eroding trust in the brand. It is likely that the brand damage would have been less severe if Samsung had managed to navigate these retailer issues more effectively. Conversely, opting for a lesser investment in the product recall could have intensified the brand damage significantly.
>
> Despite Samsung's efforts to provide replacements and improve safety measures, the recall had longer-term consequences. It took considerable time for Samsung to recover its brand from this incident (see Fig. 4.4).
>
> The Galaxy Note 7 recall emphasized the critical importance of quality control and product safety in the technology sector. It underscored the necessity for prompt and transparent action during a product recall, as well as effective collaboration between manufacturers and retailers to ensure the recall process's success.

Fig. 4.3 Message to and return instructions for the Samsung Galaxy Note 7 owners. Sources: Image snapshot from YouTube video (youtube.com/watch?v=U13sOLHG8Dg), Safety recall notice cited after Samsung (2016)

Finally, managers must also consider another often neglected aspect during product recalls: *resale platforms* like eBay, Etsy, and Facebook. Companies should also keep a close eye on such resale platforms, as many consumers, either unaware of product recalls or disregarding safety concerns, continue to sell recalled items. This poses a serious risk, as unsuspecting buyers may mistakenly believe these products are safe.

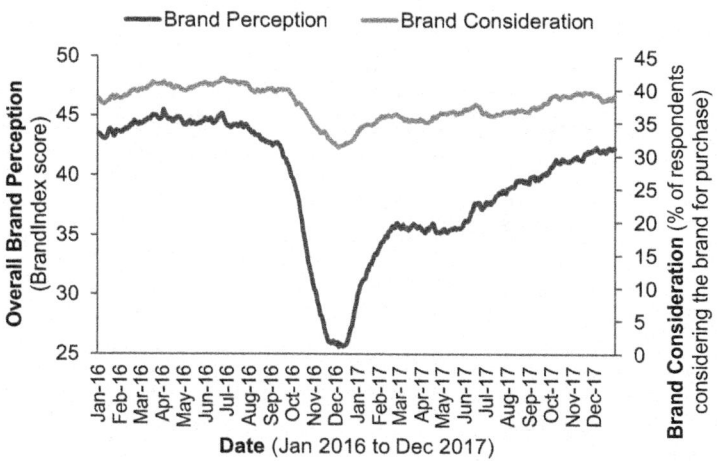

Fig. 4.4 Brand perception and brand consideration for Samsung brand in the USA 2016–2017. Source: Own illustration based on data from YouGov BrandIndex

For example, the Fisher-Price Rock 'n Play sleeper has been associated with the tragic deaths of approximately 100 infants, with around 70 of these incidents occurring *after* the product was initially recalled in 2019. One contributing factor is that the product remained available online despite its recall, underscoring the inadequacy of monitoring procedures on resale platforms (abc7, 2023).

While manufacturers are not directly responsible for resale platforms, incidents involving recalled products being sold secondhand can significantly harm brand reputations. Therefore, it is crucial for manufacturers not to rely solely on chronically underfunded and understaffed regulatory agencies to monitor resale platforms. Instead, they should take proactive steps to engage with these platforms, communicating recalls and collaborating on monitoring efforts. This proactive approach is essential for protecting consumers and upholding brand integrity.

4.3 Public Policymakers and Regulators

Public policymakers and regulators play crucial roles in product recalls, ensuring companies adhere to safety standards and regulations while safeguarding customers' welfare. Their responsibilities encompass overseeing the recall process, enforcing legal compliance, and fostering communication among all stakeholders.

For companies, engaging with policymakers and regulators during a product recall entails various critical aspects. The following example highlights the potential consequences firms may encounter from regulators if they disregard regulations.

> **The Peloton Tread+ Treadmill Safety Incident**
> In 2023, the U.S. Consumer Product Safety Commission (CPSC) unveiled a significant case involving Peloton Interactive Inc. (CPSC, 2023). The company consented to a civil penalty of $19,065,000 following charges brought forth by the CPSC. These charges allege that Peloton failed to promptly report to the CPSC, as mandated by law, regarding defects discovered in its Tread+ treadmill. These defects posed a significant product hazard and presented an unreasonable risk of serious injury to consumers, particularly children (see Fig. 4.5).
>
> The case originated from incidents reported to Peloton starting in December 2018 and extending into 2019, concerning pull-under and entrapment issues in the rear of the treadmills, resulting in injuries. Despite being aware of these incidents, Peloton did not promptly report them to the CPSC. Upon eventually filing a report with the CPSC, there were over 150 accounts of individuals, pets, and objects being pulled under the rear of the Tread+ treadmill, resulting in one child's fatality and 13 injuries, including broken bones and lacerations. Furthermore, Peloton faced accusations of knowingly distributing 38 recalled Tread+ treadmills *following* the public announcement of the recall.
>
> Possibly spurred by Peloton's very defensive response to the serious safety incident, regulatory authorities (CPSC), escalated their measures, even resorting to releasing videos on popular Internet platforms like Facebook and YouTube to alert consumers (refer Fig. 4.5). The YouTube video alone garnered nearly 1.5 million views. This case vividly illustrates the influential role regulators can play in exerting pressure on companies that resist cooperation and compliance.
>
> As part of the settlement, Peloton agreed to implement an enhanced compliance program and internal controls to ensure future adherence to the U.S. Consumer Product Safety Act (CPSA). Additionally, the company has been mandated to file annual reports regarding its compliance program and internal controls for a period of 5 years.

Adhering to relevant laws and regulations is paramount. In most countries, companies cannot initiate a product recall without first informing the authorities and securing their approval. This entails adhering to

4 The Roles of Different Stakeholder Groups 55

Fig. 4.5 Peloton Tread+ Treadmill Safety Incident. Source: Snapshot from YouTube video (youtube.com/watch?v=onXNnICYJ4Y&rco=1)

reporting requirements, following notification procedures, and implementing remediation efforts outlined by regulatory bodies. Maintaining transparent communication with regulatory bodies is equally crucial during a recall. Companies should uphold openness and honesty regarding the defect's nature, the scope of the recall, and the measures taken to rectify the issue. Clear and accurate communication fosters trust with regulators.

Furthermore, collaboration with policymakers and regulators is essential. Companies should closely cooperate with these stakeholders, offering access to information and resources to facilitate oversight, enforcement, and legislative efforts. Such cooperation ensures a synchronized response to the recall and addresses any concerns regulators may raise. Proactively engaging with policymakers and regulators demonstrates a dedication to resolving the issue and safeguarding customers. Seeking guidance and input from these stakeholders reflects respect for their expertise and assists in refining recall strategies and actions. Ultimately, regulators prioritize customer safety.

Despite the necessity of collaboration, companies may encounter challenges when working with policymakers and regulators. However, offering clear guidelines is challenging due to regulators' surprising disconnect not only between countries but also within them (Ball et al., 2022). Navigating the complex regulatory landscape surrounding product recalls can be daunting, especially for companies operating in multiple jurisdictions with varying requirements. Non-compliance with regulations can result in legal risks, including potential litigation and regulatory penalties (see Sect. 3.1), as illustrated by the Peloton case above. Therefore, comprehending and adhering to all applicable laws is vital to avoid legal consequences.

Resource constraints, such as limited staff or expertise, may hinder companies' ability to effectively engage with policymakers and regulators during a recall. Additionally, failure to cooperate with regulators or comply with regulations can tarnish a company's reputation, impacting customer trust and brand reputation in the long term.

Despite these challenges, effective collaboration with policymakers and regulators is essential for successfully managing product recalls. By prioritizing customer safety, compliance, transparency, cooperation, and proactive engagement, companies can navigate the complexities of the recall process and regulations.

4.4 Suppliers

In the realm of product recall management, suppliers play diverse roles that manufacturers must grasp to ensure a seamless and efficient recall process. The duties of suppliers can vary based on contract terms, industry norms, and legal frameworks. In certain scenarios, suppliers may have contractual obligations to share in recall expenses, particularly if faulty components or materials they provided are linked to the issue. Compliance with pertinent legal provisions and recall regulations is also part of suppliers' responsibilities, which may involve direct communication with authorities or liaising with manufacturers.

Above all, suppliers bear the responsibility of promptly notifying manufacturers about potential defects or safety concerns in the components or materials they supply. However, companies hold significant sway over whether suppliers actually report such issues. It is crucial to assuage suppliers' fears of damaging contractual ties by reporting problems within their purview. This phenomenon, known as the *MUM effect* (Minimizing Unpleasant Message effect; Coombs, 2022), can lead suppliers to remain silent, conceal, or downplay issues out of fear of repercussions for errors. Similarly, pressuring suppliers is counterproductive.

Another critical aspect relates to how manufacturers receive and handle information. The following example underscores the potentially disastrous outcomes of the MUM effect. However, in this scenario, the blame lies less with the supplier and more with the manufacturer of the final product—such as a space rocket—who downplayed issues to avoid delaying the launch, then shifted blame to the supplier for not clearly communicating the problem, despite the supplier having issued a warning signal.

The Space Shuttle Challenger Disaster

On January 28, 1986, NASA's Space Shuttle Challenger met a tragic fate as it exploded during launch, claiming the lives of all seven crew members. The primary culprit behind this disaster was pinpointed to be the failure of O-rings in the solid rocket boosters to operate effectively in low temperatures. These O-rings, crucial for sealing, were intended to prevent the leakage of fuel gases (Kim, 2020).

The supplier of these sealing rings, Morton Thiokol, played an important role in this tragic incident. In the days preceding the launch, engineers at Morton Thiokol voiced concerns about the anticipated low temperatures on the launch day. They feared that the elasticity of the seals might be compromised in the cold, potentially leading to failure. Allan McDonald, the director of the Space Shuttle Solid Rocket Motor Project at Morton Thiokol, declined to endorse a launch recommendation for the Challenger. Despite these warnings and against the engineers' advice, NASA opted to proceed with the launch, influenced by pressure and time constraints. The chilly conditions on the morning of the launch ultimately led to the failure of the sealing rings, resulting in the shuttle's explosion (see Fig. 4.6).

Following the Challenger disaster, NASA faced intense scrutiny and backlash for its decision-making processes and safety measures. This tragic event spurred a thorough investigation led by the Rogers Commission, uncovering systemic flaws in NASA's organizational culture and communication channels. Consequently, NASA implemented significant reforms aimed at bolstering safety protocols, including the establishment of a dedicated safety oversight office and a reevaluation of risk assessment procedures.

This devastating incident underscores the utmost importance of open communication between suppliers and manufacturers, as well as the imperative to address safety concerns promptly. It served as a stark reminder of the significance of transparency and accountability in the supply chain, particularly when dealing with components critical to safety.

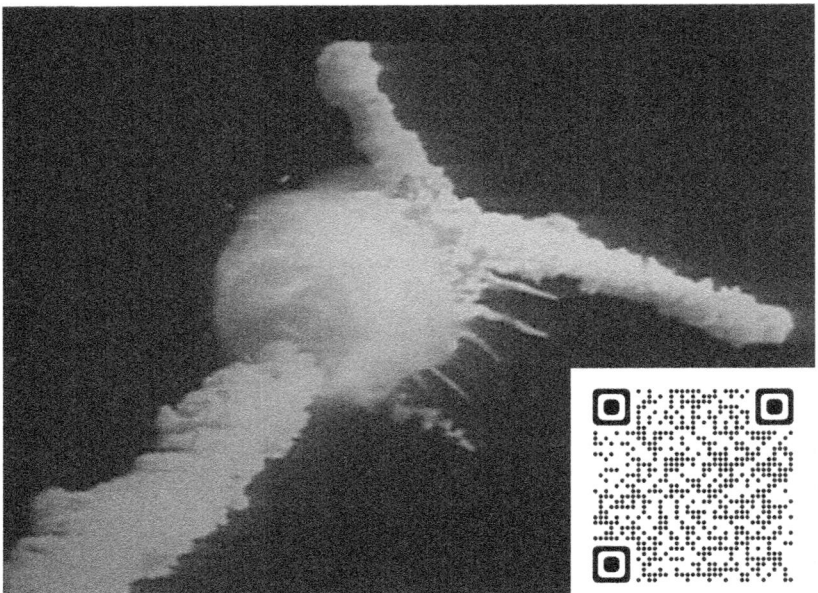

Fig. 4.6 Space Shuttle Challenger disaster. Source: Snapshot from YouTube video (youtube.com/watch?v=yibNEcn-4yQ)

The timely reporting of product issues by the supplier lays the foundation for the manufacturer's swift response. Suppliers should be actively engaged in both the planning and execution of recall measures to ensure the situation is handled efficiently. Moreover, suppliers play a pivotal role in furnishing comprehensive information about affected products, including batch analysis and root cause investigations.

Throughout the recall process, suppliers can provide valuable assistance by identifying affected batches, tracking components, or offering logistical support for returns. However, the flow of information along the supply chain, effective monitoring and quality control, as well as prompt action in response to issues, cannot be assumed—as every small detail can carry significant consequences. Even a minor labeling error can lead to tragic outcomes, as illustrated in the following example.

> **Mislabeled Vanilla Florentine Cookies**
> In January 2024, a young dancer tragically lost her life after consuming a cookie containing peanuts, despite having a severe peanut allergy (Kim, 2024). The woman suffered an anaphylactic shock due to a severe allergic reaction (Deliso, 2024). The absence of allergen information on the package's ingredient list was identified as the cause of this tragedy. The product in question, "Vanilla Florentine Cookies," was sold at Stew Leonard's stores in the USA from early November to late December 2023. The specific batch was promptly recalled in collaboration with the U.S. Food and Drug Administration (FDA) (Sleter, 2024).
> Accountability for this terrible incident is questioned, with Stew Leonard Jr., the CEO, acknowledging in a video message shortly after the event that the supplier had substituted peanuts for soy nuts without informing safety personnel. In contrast, Cookies United, the supplier, accused Stew Leonard's of using an outdated and incorrect ingredient list after repackaging the cookies at their facilities under the Stew Leonard's brand name. Cookies United asserted that they had notified Stew Leonard's in July 2023 that the product contained peanuts, and all packages were properly labeled. Ultimately, the courts will determine the party responsible for this error, likely resulting in reputation damage for both companies.
> This tragic case emphasizes the crucial importance of monitoring the supply chain and maintaining continuous information exchange throughout, in both directions, to detect or prevent problems at an early stage.

In conclusion, a seamless flow of information, continual monitoring, and stringent quality control, coupled with a trusting relationship between suppliers and manufacturers, are essential for swiftly detecting product failures and ensuring the effectiveness of the recall process. Establishing clear agreements and protocols among all stakeholders beforehand is pivotal for promptly and cohesively addressing issues during a product recall. This proactive approach helps mitigate potential risks and preserves the integrity of the supply chain and the recall process.

4.5 Media

The media, including social media, and opinion leaders/influencers, play pivotal roles in product recall management on multiple fronts. They serve as intermediaries who organize much of the information flow to various stakeholders (Vogler et al., 2016). Initially, a product failure becomes a matter of public interest due to the potential impact on public health and the deviation from expectations toward manufacturers and retailers of selling reliable and safe products. Sometimes, companies become aware of a product failure for the first time through the media. The ensuing public interest in the product failure, as per the Agenda-setting Theory (McCombs & Shaw, 1972), leads to increased coverage in the (social) media, shaping its significance and raising public awareness.

This presents a dual-edged impact for the company. On one hand, it helps in notifying customers, retailers, and wholesalers about the product failure, thereby contributing to a more effective recall management—provided the company promptly issues the recall (Heidari & Raithel, 2024). However, on the other hand, it also draws attention to the product failure and recall among stakeholders not directly affected by the recall. This heightened awareness may sow uncertainty and skepticism among other customers, potential buyers, and actors in the financial markets regarding the quality and reliability of the company's products beyond those being recalled.

The potential negative impact on these stakeholders emerges when the media coverage of the recall story emphasizes values and facts that fuel this uncertainty and skepticism. To address this, the company should engage with the media proactively instead of resorting to defensive strategies like stonewalling or downplaying the issue. Anticipating and actively managing the situation "in real time" is crucial for navigating the challenges posed by media coverage during a product recall. A classic example illustrating this recommendation is potentially one of the earliest social media *firestorms* in history.

How a Pen Almost Locked Down Kryptonite

In 2004, Kryptonite, a well-respected bicycle lock manufacturer, faced a significant product failure when a YouTube video demonstrated how easily their popular tubular cylinder locks could be unlocked using a basic Bic pen (BikeBiz, 2005). The video quickly went viral, capturing widespread attention and raising serious concerns about the security of Kryptonite locks. Figure 4.7 includes both the link and QR code directing to the original video. This "trick" was replicated by numerous others who shared their successful attempts on the Internet.

However, the media played a crucial role in amplifying the impact of this product failure, with the YouTube platform facilitating the rapid spread of the vulnerability to a large audience. This social media firestorm swiftly grabbed the attention of traditional news outlets, extending its reach even further. Kryptonite's response to the crisis was notably slow and insufficient. Unaware of the video at first, the company took five business days before issuing any response, a delay that contradicts recommended crisis management timelines.

Research suggests that when faced with negative news, a company should ideally respond within 24 h (the "golden 24 hours rule") and no later than 48 h after the incident (e.g., Hock & Raithel, 2020). The consequences of Kryptonite's sluggish response were severe. The widespread exposure of the vulnerability tarnished the company's reputation for producing secure and reliable bike locks. For days, customers were left uncertain about whether their products were affected and what steps to take, eroding trust in the brand. This resulted in a significant wave of negative publicity and backlash, inflicting substantial financial losses on Kryptonite that surpassed the costs associated with the recall and replacement of over 400,000 locks in 21 countries.

This incident underscores the influential role of social media in shaping public perceptions and highlights the critical importance for companies to respond promptly and transparently to product failures. In today's era of instant information dissemination, proactive measures are vital for promptly addressing and rectifying issues, thereby mitigating potential damage to both reputation and financial standing.

On a notable side note, the firestorm did not arise unexpectedly. In fact, Kryptonite had at least 12 years to address the structural vulnerability of its tubular cylinder lock system, as the issue had been previously highlighted as early as 1992 in the New Cyclist magazine and a BBC consumer-rights program (Cheney, 2004). However, this revelation eventually faded from public awareness.

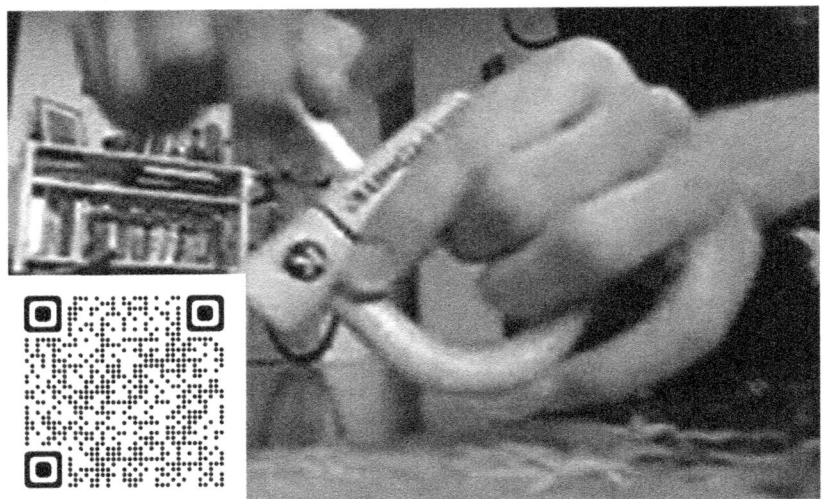

Fig. 4.7 Opening a Kryptonite New York Disc Lock using a Bic ballpoint pen. Source: Snapshot from YouTube video (youtube.com/watch?v=HAiu3pMI7D0)

One common mistake companies often make is adopting a stance of stonewalling and refusing to engage with journalists investigating product failures or subsequent recalls. However, research shows that such defensive behavior and stonewalling usually backfire:

A journalist who uncovered significant wrongdoing by a company stated (cited after Koehler & Raithel, 2018: 522): "If an organisation offends against regulations or against ethical principles on purpose, then I am especially interested in such a case. In addition, I also had a sense of foreboding that this would not be everything. The scope of the issue really seemed to be huge." This conviction was further reinforced by the organization's lack of transparent engagement with the media, opting instead to manipulate media coverage, suggesting that the organization may have something to hide.

Another journalist, also involved in this revelation, explained that when an organization boasts a clean and stellar image, as in this case, the crisis becomes especially newsworthy and motivates journalists to dig deeper (cited after Koehler & Raithel, 2018: 522): "It's just more 'fun' to scratch on untainted images and moral crusaders." However, this journalist also stressed that the prior relationship with a company plays a significant role (cited after Koehler & Raithel, 2018: 522): "If the company engaged in building a trustful relationship before the crisis occurred - such as by proactive contact - then this favorable relationship will have spillover effects on my future media reports." Consequently, it becomes unmistakably clear that embracing a proactive and collaborative approach with the media is indispensable.

4.6 Investors and Financial Analysts

During a product recall, investors and financial analysts evaluate the financial implications on the company (Raithel & Hock, 2021; Li et al., 2024). They assess how the recall impacts revenue, profitability, and shareholder value, taking into account various factors such as recall costs, potential litigation expenses, and the repercussions on future sales and market share.

Additionally, investors and financial analysts closely monitor the company's reputation management throughout the recall process. They scrutinize how the company's response to the recall influences brand reputation and consumer trust, evaluating the public's perception of transparency and communication with stakeholders.

Operational performance also garners significant attention from investors and financial analysts during a recall. They analyze the company's proficiency in managing logistics, addressing customer inquiries, and facilitating product replacements or refunds with efficiency and effectiveness. This includes assessing response times, process efficiency, and customer satisfaction levels.

Moreover, regulatory compliance is a crucial concern for investors and financial analysts. They evaluate whether the company complies with reporting obligations, cooperates with regulatory authorities, and implements corrective actions to prevent similar incidents in the future. Maintaining compliance with regulations is vital for mitigating legal risks and upholding investor confidence.

Finally, investors and financial analysts consider the company's long-term sustainability in light of the recall. They scrutinize the company's resilience, adaptability, and recovery strategies post-crisis, as well as its initiatives to prevent recurrence of similar incidents. This comprehensive evaluation significantly influences investor decisions and stock prices, thereby impacting the company's overall financial stability and market position.

> **The Johnson & Johnson Phantom Recall**
> In 2010, Johnson & Johnson, the healthcare giant, faced criticism over its handling of a recall involving several popular over-the-counter drugs, notably a "phantom recall" of Motrin (Perrone, 2010). This unconventional approach involved a subcontractor quietly purchasing Motrin from drug stores instead of issuing an immediate recall and informing consumers about potential product issues. Despite this controversy, investors showed limited concern, as Johnson & Johnson's shares traded only 6% below their 52-week high. The recall prompted congressional scrutiny, leading to CEO Bill Weldon testifying about the company's actions, acknowledging that they "let the public down."
> In contrast to other companies hit by scandals, such as Toyota in 2010, Johnson & Johnson avoided a significant stock sell-off. This resilience could be attributed to the absence of reported illnesses linked to the recalled products. Despite investigative reporting uncovering concerning patterns, including Berkshire Hathaway's increased stake in the company, investors remained relatively unfazed. They focused on the company's diverse product portfolio, strong franchises, and stable dividend yield of 3.5%, factors that bolstered their confidence in Johnson & Johnson's ability to weather the recall storm. As long as overall sales and profits remained steady, Johnson & Johnson's stock was anticipated to maintain favorability on Wall Street.
> Moreover, investors recognized Johnson & Johnson's historical proficiency in crisis management, notably during the Tylenol cyanide scare of 1982. During this crisis, the company promptly responded by recalling millions of bottles of Tylenol and implementing tamper-resistant packaging, setting a precedent for corporate crisis management. Their transparent communication, swift action, and commitment to consumer safety garnered praise and established a benchmark for effective crisis response in the corporate world.

For companies, the involvement of investors and financial analysts during a recall highlights the importance of proactive and transparent management of the recall process. It is crucial for companies to prioritize effective communication with financial market actors by providing regular updates on the recall's status and demonstrating their commitment to resolving the issue. Additionally, companies must ensure smooth operational performance throughout the recall to minimize disruptions and uphold customer satisfaction. This involves implementing streamlined processes for logistics, handling customer inquiries, and managing product replacements or refunds.

Maintaining regulatory compliance is paramount for companies to mitigate legal risks and uphold investor confidence. Compliance entails adhering to reporting obligations, collaborating with regulatory authorities, and taking corrective actions to prevent future incidents. Furthermore, companies should focus on long-term sustainability by implementing strategic initiatives to prevent similar incidents in the future. This may include investing in product safety measures, enhancing quality control processes, and bolstering risk management protocols.

Overall, companies must acknowledge the critical role of investors and financial analysts in assessing the impact of a recall and take proactive steps to address their concerns. By prioritizing transparency, operational efficiency, regulatory compliance, and long-term sustainability, companies can effectively mitigate the financial and reputational risks associated with product recalls.

References

abc7. (2023, August 30). *Congressman calls on online platforms to remove recalled products linked to infant death*. Retrieved April 15, 2024, from https://abc7ny.com/infant-recall-product-facebook/13715664/.

Anwyl, J. (2016, September 29). The Samsung galaxy note 7 recall: T-mobile has not thought through their process. Forbes. Retrieved April 15, 2024, from https://www.forbes.com/sites/jeremyanwyl/2016/09/29/the-samsung-galaxy-note-7-recall-t-mobile-has-not-thought-through-their-process/.

Ball, G. P., Wowak, K. D., & Mukherjee, U. K. (2022). Product recall research: Dimensions, methods, and regulator implications. In *Tutorials in operations research: Emerging and impactful topics in operations* (pp. 116–132). INFORMS.

BikeBiz. (2005, January 27). *Kryptonite awarded with "Dumbest Moment of 2004" by US mag*. Retrieved April 15, 2024, from https://bikebiz.com/kryptonite-awarded-with-dumbest-moment-of-2004-by-us-mag/.

Cave, C. (2017, August 10). CPSC defect recall data. Slideshare. Retrieved April 21, 2024, from https://www.slideshare.net/slideshow/cpsc-recall-effectiveness-workshop-recall-data/78744492. Accessed April 21, 2024.

CBS. (2014). *GM uses facebook, phone calls to get recalled cars fixed*. Retrieved April 15, 2024, from https://www.cbsnews.com/newyork/news/gm-uses-facebook-phone-calls-to-get-recalled-cars-fixed/.

Cheney, P. (2004, September 24). Class-action lawsuit hinges on bike locks. *The Globe and Mail*. Retrieved April 15, 2024, from https://www.theglobeandmail.com/news/national/class-action-lawsuit-hinges-on-bike-locks/article18273601/.

Consumer Product Safety Commission. (2023). *Peloton agrees to pay $19 million civil penalty for failure to immediately report tread+ treadmill entrapment hazards and for distributing recalled treadmills*. Retrieved April 15, 2024, from https://www.cpsc.gov/Newsroom/News-Releases/2023/Peloton-Agrees-to-Pay-19-Million-Civil-Penalty-for-Failure-to-Immediately-Report-Tread-Treadmill-Entrapment-Hazards-and-for-Distributing-Recalled-Treadmills.

Coombs, W. T. (2022). *Ongoing crisis communication: Planning, managing, and responding* (6th ed.).

Deliso, M. (2024, January 26). Woman, 25, dies from allergic reaction after eating mislabeled cookies with peanuts from Stew Leonard's. *ABC News*. Retrieved March 16, 2024, from https://abcnews.go.com/US/stew-leonards-peanut-cookies-death/story?id=106679296.

Heidari & Raithel (2024). The effects of media coverage during product harm crisis on product recall effectiveness. Proceedings of the European Marketing Academy, 53rd.

Hock, S. J., & Raithel, S. (2020). Managing negative celebrity endorser publicity: How announcements of firm (non) responses affect stock returns. *Management Science, 66*(3), 1473–1495.

Kim, A. (2020, January 28). 34 years ago today, the space shuttle challenger broke apart and killed everyone on board. CNN. Retrieved April 15, 2024, from https://edition.cnn.com/2020/01/28/us/space-shuttle-challenger-34-years-scn-trnd/index.html#:~:text=The%20space%20shuttle%20Challenger%20appeared%20to%20have%20exploded%20after%20a%20fireball%20ignited.&text=The%20Challenger%20broke%20apart%2073,across%20the%20US%20that%20morning.

Kim, C. (2024, January 26). Órla Baxendale: Dancer with allergy eats mislabelled Stew Leonard's cookie and dies. *BBC*. Retrieved April 15, 2024, from https://www.bbc.com/news/world-us-canada-68102202.

Koehler, I., & Raithel, S. (2018). Internal, external, and media stakeholders' evaluations during transgressions. *Corporate Communications: An International Journal, 23*(4), 512–527.

Krisher, T. (2014, May 8). GM recall leaves customers frustrated and waiting. *Hendersonville Times-News*. Retrieved April 15, 2024, from https://eu.blueridgenow.com/story/news/2014/05/08/gm-recall-leaves-customers-frustrated-and-waiting/28317124007/.

Li, H., Bapuji, H., Talluri, S., & Singh, P. J. (2022). A cross-disciplinary review of product recall research: A stakeholder-stage framework. *Transportation Research Part E: Logistics and Transportation Review, 163*, 102732.

Li, Y., Lin, Y., Wang, X., & Yang, S. (2024). Wall street and product quality: The duality of analysts. *The Accounting Review, 1–34*. https://doi.org/10.2308/TAR-2022-0218

McCombs, M. E., & Shaw, D. L. (1972). The agenda-setting function of mass media. *The Public Opinion Quarterly, 36*(2), 176–187.

National Highway Traffic Safety Administration. (2014). *GM owner notification letter "Important safety recall"*. Retrieved April 22, 2024, from https://static.nhtsa.gov/odi/rcl/2014/RCONL-14V047-3498.pdf.

Perrone, M. (2010, June 1). Drug maker investigated for 'phantom recall'. *NBC News*. Retrieved April 15, 2024, from https://www.nbcnews.com/health/health-news/drug-maker-investigated-phantom-recall-flna1c9447037.

Plumer, B. (2015 May 11). The GM recall scandal of 2014. Vox. Retrieved April 15, 2024, from https://www.vox.com/2014/10/3/18073458/gm-car-recall.

Raithel, S., & Hock, S. J. (2021). The crisis-response match: An empirical investigation. *Strategic Management Journal, 42*(1), 170–184.

Samsung. (2016, September 20). *Samsung galaxy Note7 US voluntary recall update*. Retrieved April 25, 2024, from https://news.samsung.com/us/samsung-galaxy-note7-us-voluntary-recall-update-firmware-update-green-battery-icon/.

Selyukh, A. (2016, September 14). The troubled galaxy note 7 leaves some Samsung customers frustrated. NPR. Retrieved April 15, 2024, from https://www.npr.org/sections/alltechconsidered/2016/09/14/493916062/the-troubled-galaxy-note-7-leaves-some-samsung-customers-frustrated.

Sleter, G. (2024, January 26). Stew Leonard's recalls cookies following dancer's death. Store Brands. Retrieved February 8, 2024, from https://storebrands.com/stew-leonards-recalls-cookies-following-dancers-death.

Vogler, D., Schranz, M., & Eisenegger, M. (2016). Stakeholder group influence on media reputation in crisis periods. *Corporate Communications: An International Journal, 21*(3), 322–332.

5

The Product Recall Management Cycle

> **What to Expect in This Chapter**
> - This chapter provides a detailed discussion of the product management cycle, delineating its phases: pre-recall, recall, and post-recall.
> - Within the pre-recall phase, emphasis is placed on planning and recall readiness, facilitated by the establishment of a cross-functional product recalls task force, formulation of general product recall guidelines, implementation of training and education initiatives, conducting mock recall exercises, and enhancing product tracing, safety, and quality control measures.
> - The recall phase is further dissected into seven distinct sub-processes, including problem identification, risk assessment, decision on recall, recall plan creation, communication with relevant stakeholders, execution of the recall and monitoring, and documentation and reporting.
> - Transitioning into the post-recall phase, the focus shifts toward performance recovery and learning from the crisis.

Preparing for a product recall resembles a somewhat *reversed* marketing strategy: the focus shifts toward retrieving products from customers and distributors. Despite the urgency, it is crucial for the company to maintain broader marketing objectives, including preserving customer satisfaction and nurturing relationships. The expertise of the marketing department plays a vital role in orchestrating successful recalls. Therefore, assigning recall responsibility to a seasoned marketing executive—like the Chief Marketing Officer or Vice President of Marketing—ensures the organization is well-equipped to swiftly and effectively execute recall procedures, fostering a culture of *recall readiness* (Liu et al., 2023).

Effective product recall management comprises three critical phases. At its core is the product-harm crisis and the recall process itself, constituting the *recall phase* (Sect. 5.2). This phase is marked by uncertainty and time sensitivity, necessitating prompt decisions under pressure (Wowak et al., 2022). Therefore, strategic planning beforehand and ensuring organizational readiness are essential components of the *pre-recall phase* (Sect. 5.1). After completing the recall, insights gained should inform improved planning and preparation for future recalls, representing the *post-recall phase* (Sect. 5.3). Figure 5.1 offers an overview of this product recall management cycle.

Throughout all phases, prioritizing the needs and roles of customers and distribution networks is paramount since the success of the recall largely depends on their perception of and compliance with the recommended actions. Other stakeholders—including regulators, policymakers, suppliers, the media, and financial market actors—play supportive roles. While they closely monitor the recall process, their concerns primarily revolve around the firm's efforts to retrieve the recalled products and maintain close relationships with customers and distributors. Effective communication with these stakeholders is crucial, but ultimately directed toward reassuring customers and users, as well as demonstrating the firm's commitment to addressing the issue at hand. The Intel case below underscores the critical significance of prioritizing a customer-centric approach during a product harm crisis.

> **How Intel Learned the Hard Way**
> The importance of adopting the perspective of customers when managing product recalls becomes evident when looking at how Intel Corporation handled defects in their Pentium processors in 1994. Customers began to report errors during complex calculations, prompting Intel's initial response to downplay and minimize the issue. Intel's customer support informed affected customers that errors were statistically improbable, with the average user encountering a problem once every 27,000 years. Intel offered replacements only to customers who could prove their work was sophisticated enough to be negatively affected (Lewis, 1994; Hearit, 1999).

However, the situation escalated when IBM announced a halt to shipments of computers with Intel's Pentium processors a couple of weeks later. IBM criticized Intel for significantly underestimating the likelihood of calculation errors due to the defect. This news caused Intel's stock to plummet, leading to a temporary halt in trading (Ramirez, 1994). In response, Intel changed its recall strategy from minimizing the defect to issuing a public apology to its customers. The company offered free replacements for all defective processors (Corcoran, 1994).

In hindsight, Intel's CEO admitted to *The Wall Street Journal* that the company became too focused on a fact-based analysis of the issue and neglected to consider the emotional aspect of customer concerns. Customers felt unheard as Intel minimized the risks and dictated their perceptions (Carlton & Yoder, 1994). This oversight proved costly for Intel, with the overall costs of the recall estimated at $500 million (Smith et al., 1996).

The following case study, provided by Sedgwick—the world's leading product recall company—underlines the importance of putting the customer into the center of product recall management efforts and of aligning customers' needs with regulatory requirements.

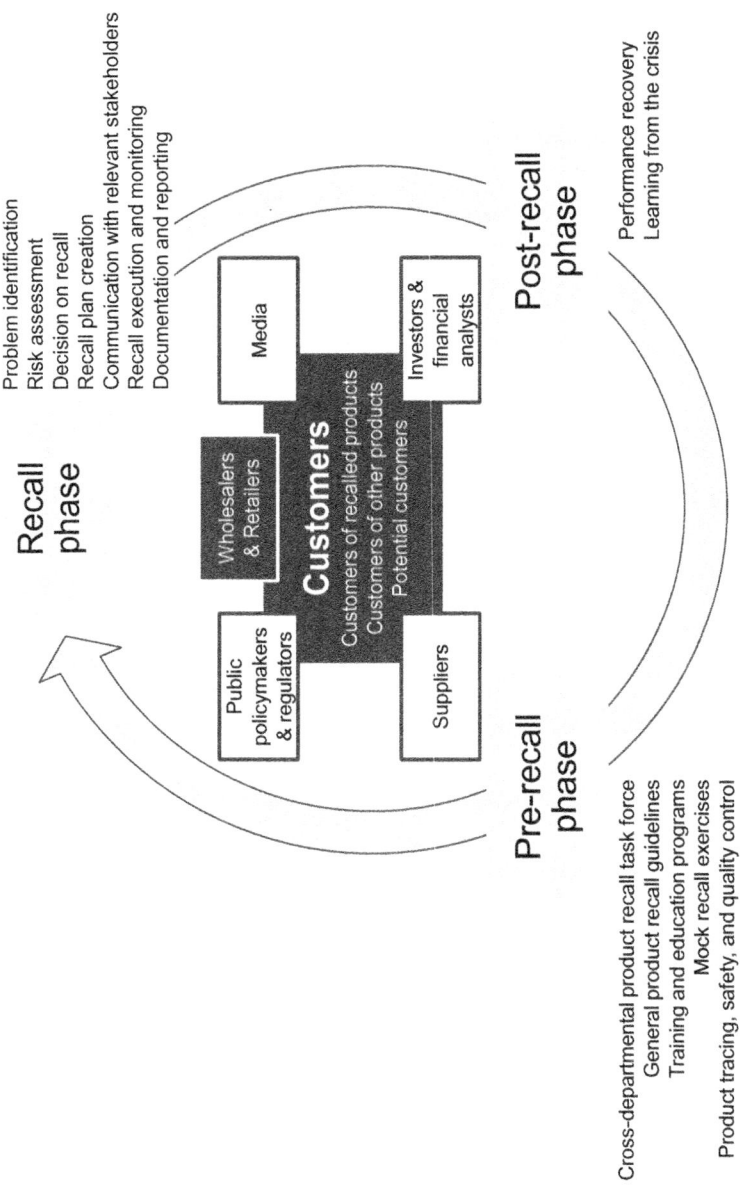

Fig. 5.1 The product recall management cycle. Source: Own illustration

Case Study: How a Customized Approach to Global Recall Management Yielded Results

Chris Harvey, Sr. Vice President, Client Services—Sedgwick Brand Protection[1]

Introduction

Brand and reputation are the most valuable and vulnerable assets a business has. Brands embody and encapsulate everything a business does, and its customers expect. Nothing says more about a company's commitment to its customers than its efforts to uphold promises of safety, quality, and service. That is why companies are often remembered more for how they handle an in-market challenge than for the problem itself.

Historically, recalls were localized events, confined to specific geographies and governed by a single regulatory jurisdiction. However, with the globalization of economies and increased partnerships among regulators regarding product safety concerns, the recall management landscape has become significantly more complex. This evolution has heightened both operational and reputational risks for companies navigating the intricate maze of international regulations and standards.

Consider the recall of a popular electronic device powered by a lithium-ion battery, which sold over two million units of a specific model across more than 80 countries to consumers speaking 11 languages. Over the course of the product's lifecycle, the United States-based manufacturer received an increasing number of publicized reports of minor injuries resulting from a battery issue that caused the device to overheat. As the company's product safety record came under regulatory and public scrutiny, the brand faced escalating reputational risks.

Defining the Challenges

Given the global nature of the product, numerous regulators were involved, each invested in ensuring the recall was not only compliant but effective. Each regulatory body had its own requirements for recall management and product handling, directly impacting the company's ability to notify, engage and offer remedies to impacted consumers.

---

[1] For three decades, companies of all sizes and sectors have trusted Sedgwick Brand Protection's expertise in preparing for and resolving their product-related challenges. Since 1995, Sedgwick has successfully managed more than 7,000 of the most sensitive and time-critical product recall programs, spanning 100 countries and 50 languages. From recall-readiness audits and mock recall simulations, to complete turn-key retrieval and remediation solutions—including regulatory guidance and reporting, sedgwick has the experience and resources to manage a company's product wherever it is in market. To discover more, visit: www.sedgwick.com/brandprotection.

The company was unprepared to handle the logistical demands of a battery-related recall in a regulatory-compliant manner. Compounding the challenge, the manufacturer relied heavily on retail partners, making a unified approach to remedy management unfeasible. Retailers were not universally equipped to handle returns and the company lacked the infrastructure to ship products outside of the United States.

Communication and remedy management also presented significant challenges. While consumers in the continental United States were able to return the recalled device to a retail store or return via post using a compliant mailing package, an alternative solution was needed in the remaining 80 countries. Further complicating matters, the impacted products lacked a visible identifier, preventing the manufacturer from limiting the scope of the recall or ensuring that only one refund or remedy was issued per unit. Consequently, the risk of fraudulent claims was high.

Finding the Solutions

The manufacturer sought support from Sedgwick's brand protection division, a global leader in product recall solutions. Through this partnership, the device manufacturer gained access to a comprehensive portfolio of end-to-end recall solutions, best-in-class experience, and expertise in navigating the stringent regulatory requirements for Damaged, Defective, or Recalled (DDR) lithium batteries. From a scalable website in 11 languages, and online product registration to secure financial transactions, the company was able to deliver the necessary remedies while mitigating the risk of fraud.

In the United States, consumers were able to order a compliant postal return kit and safely return their devices. The return kit adhered to all Department of Transportation requirements for packaging, permit, and labeling. Upon receipt, the returns were processed and validated, after which a reimbursement was issued that could be used to purchase a replacement device.

However, a similar postal return process was not feasible outside the United States due to regulatory requirements for the transport and disposal of lithium-ion batteries. Fortunately, since the device required owner setup upon first use, associated account information could be used to verify ownership, issue refunds, and help reduce fraud. To accomplish this, the recall website enabled consumers to validate impacted units using online credentials confirmed by the manufacturer. This approach ensured that a registered serial number could only be used to obtain the financial incentive once. Upon validation, consumers receive instructions on how to return or destroy the unit based on local regulations. Reimbursement then promptly followed.

Delivering the Results

A recall of this magnitude demands significant resources to manage even just the consumer touchpoints, including over 260,000 calls in 11 languages, more than one million product registrations, and multiple reimbursement types across different currencies and geographies.

This strategy enabled a tailored approach to consumer engagement by region, offering not only language-specific support but also multiple electronic and physical options for receiving accurate refunds and customized instructions for product disposal.

Product handling added complexity, requiring specialized expertise for managing DDR lithium battery shipments within the continental United States, and guidance for compliant products storage, recycling, and disposal across 80 countries. However, leveraging experts with global experience led to success.

This expertise enabled the company to manage the recall notification, product handling, remedy, and disposal process effectively and compliantly. Additionally, the extra resources allowed the company to refocus its attention on other core business objectives, including other prominent products within its portfolio.

Reviewing the Key Takeaways

While the manufacturer gained many valuable lessons that will serve it well for future product remediations and recall events, this case provides significant insights for companies evaluating their recall preparedness. Consider these among the top lessons:

- Understanding the current regulations and restrictions in every jurisdiction you operate or sell products is critical for rapid response and effective recall management.
- Regulatory compliance and customer experience go hand in hand. By prioritizing compliance and putting your customer first in all interactions, trust will remain, and customers will remain loyal.
- Do not hesitate to ask for help. Engaging a partner with global call center capabilities, logistics, and reimbursement solutions demonstrates a commitment to customized communication and solutions across all jurisdictions. This approach ensures positive customer experiences even in the most challenging circumstances.
- Mitigating fraud risk is possible. For products that may exist in multiples within a single household, delivering remedies while preventing fraud requires a delicate balance. Collaborating with a partner who understands the need to meet both objectives simultaneously helps achieve both financial and reputational goals.

In the following sections, we thoroughly explore each of the three phases while maintaining a customer-centric perspective. We delineate the challenges intrinsic to each phase and offer actionable recommendations to skillfully overcome them. By directly confronting and resolving these challenges, organizations can bolster their capacity to effectively manage product recalls and preserve strong customer relationships amidst product harm crisis.

5.1 Pre-Recall Phase: Planning and Recall Readiness

Product recalls pose a significant challenge for organizations, encompassing intricate logistics, legal intricacies, and the risk of reputational harm. It is crucial for companies to be well prepared for such situations by implementing effective frameworks and procedures.

The airline sector, renowned for its stringent oversight and regulations, serves as a prime example of crisis management excellence on a global scale. This industry sets high standards for readiness, especially in facing worst-case scenarios like airplane accidents, which could have devastating consequences. Below, we delve into the standard protocols and strategies employed by the airline industry to brace for such emergencies.

> **Airline industry's Crisis Preparedness as Tested Benchmark**
> Major airlines have developed elaborated plans and procedures to effectively manage crisis events, notably airplane crashes. These plans and procedures comprise three key elements:
>
> 1. Training Programs:
> Airlines conduct comprehensive training programs for flight crews, ground staff, and emergency response teams to prepare them for various emergency scenarios, including crashes. These programs typically cover:
>
> - Emergency procedures: Crew members are trained extensively on emergency procedures, including evacuations, fire suppression, and emergency communication protocols.
> - Aircraft familiarization: Crew members receive training on the layout and features of different aircraft types to facilitate efficient response in crash situations.

- First aid and medical training: Crew members are trained in basic first aid and medical response techniques to provide assistance to passengers and crew members in need.
- Crisis communication: Training includes effective communication techniques to ensure clear and timely communication with passengers, authorities, and other stakeholders during a crash scenario.
- Psychological support: Crew members receive training on providing psychological support to passengers and fellow crew members in the aftermath of a crash.

2. "How-To" Handbooks:

Airlines develop detailed handbooks or manuals that summarize standardized procedures for responding to crash scenarios. These handbooks, often referred to as "crisis response manuals" or "emergency procedures manuals," provide step-by-step guidance on:

- Initial response actions: Procedures for crew members to follow immediately after a crash, including securing the aircraft, initiating emergency evacuations, and contacting emergency services.
- Communication protocols: Guidelines for communicating with passengers, authorities, media, and other stakeholders during a crash scenario, including scripted messages and contact information.
— Evacuation procedures: Instructions for coordinating passenger evacuation, including prioritizing exits, deploying evacuation slides, and directing passengers to assembly points.
- Medical response: Procedures for providing first aid and medical assistance to injured passengers and crew members, including accessing medical supplies and coordinating with emergency medical services.
- Post-crash support: Guidelines for providing support and assistance to passengers, crew members, and their families in the aftermath of a crash, including access to counseling services and assistance with travel arrangements.

3. Mock Exercises:

Airlines conduct regular mock exercises or drills to test and validate their response procedures and protocols in simulated crash scenarios. These exercises involve:

- Scenario development: Designing realistic crash scenarios based on potential risks and hazards, including factors such as weather conditions, aircraft type, and location.
- Participant engagement: Involving flight crews, ground staff, emergency response teams, and other relevant personnel in the mock exercises to simulate real-life response scenarios.

> – Execution and evaluation: Conducting the mock exercises according to predefined objectives and criteria, followed by a thorough debriefing and evaluation of performance.
> – Continuous improvement: Using insights from mock exercises to identify areas for improvement in procedures, training programs, and equipment, and implementing corrective actions as needed.
>
> By investing in rigorous training programs, developing comprehensive handbooks, and conducting regular mock exercises, airlines ensure that their personnel are well prepared to respond effectively to crash scenarios, minimizing harm and maximizing safety for passengers and crew members.

Drawing from established practices in the airline industry and insights from product recall management research (e.g., Smith et al., 1996), we have devised a comprehensive framework consisting of five essential components vital for achieving recall readiness (refer Table 5.1):

1. Formation of cross-departmental product recall task force.
2. Formulation of general product recall guidelines.
3. Recall training and education program.
4. Execution of mock recall exercises.
5. Augmentation of product tracing, safety, and quality assurance measures.

In the subsequent Sects. 5.1.1–5.1.5, we elaborate on each of these five components and underlying activities.

5.1.1 Cross-Departmental Product Recall Task Force

A pivotal aspect of recall readiness involves establishing a dedicated task force comprised members from diverse departments. By consolidating expertise and responsibility within a specialized team, organizations can streamline recall management processes, reduce response times, and mitigate potential adverse effects on customers and the business.

Table 5.1 Pre-recall phase activities for achieving recall readiness

Pre-recall phase area	Activity
Cross-departmental product recall task force	– Appoint representatives from all departments and senior management – Collaborate with external advisors and specialized agencies – Assign leading role to an experienced executive with marketing expertise – Give task force responsibility for all recall-related tasks
General product recall guidelines	– Develop standardized procedures and scenarios – Document procedures in "How to"-handbook
Training and education program	– Equip employees across all departments with skills and knowledge about product safety and recall procedures
Mock recall exercises	– Test and validate recall procedures – Simulate real-life recall scenarios
Product tracing, safety, and quality control	– Establish supply chain transparency – Ensure product traceability along the whole supply chain – Conduct robust testing during product development – Perform continuous quality assurance during production – Stay informed about and comply with regulatory requirements

Source: Own illustration

This task force should encompass representatives from key areas such as purchasing, production, quality assurance, research and development, legal, marketing, corporate communications, customer service, distribution, and senior management. Additionally, involving stakeholders from specialized agencies, regulatory bodies, consumer protection organizations, and the distribution network as advisors is beneficial. Leveraging both internal and external expertise ensures the development of comprehensive recall response guidelines.

Diversity within the task force goes beyond departmental representation, extending to demographic factors. For example, research indicates that female managers approach product recalls differently from their male counterparts (Wowak et al., 2021). Therefore, a diverse task force is more likely to make balanced and thorough decisions.

The cross-departmental task force is responsible for:

- Assessing recall risks throughout the product lifecycle
- Developing and implementing recall plans and procedures
- Coordinating communication with regulatory agencies, customers, and the public
- Managing logistics related to product retrieval, replacement, or disposal
- Conducting post-recall analysis and implementing corrective actions

Collaboration with regulatory bodies and/or consulting and legal firms specializing in product compliance and recall management complements the establishment of the recall task force. This partnership is crucial as product recalls are infrequent occurrences, leaving companies lacking extensive recall management experience. Experts at the regulatory bodies as well as specialized firms provide invaluable expertise, particularly in complex scenarios involving multiple products, countries, and jurisdictions.

Ideally, this partnership should be formed *before* any recall event occurs. Firstly, the external advisor enhances recall readiness, ensuring the company is well prepared to address potential issues. Secondly, in the event of a recall, the pre-established partnership facilitates efficient recall management as the advisor is already familiar with the company's processes. This proactive approach can help to minimize disruptions and to mitigate risks.

As previously stressed, an experienced marketing executive should lead this task force or play a central role in maintaining customer-centric procedures, guidelines, and protocols. This ensures the organization's response prioritizes customer safety, satisfaction, and brand reputation alongside regulatory and operational concerns. Research indicates firms adopting a customer-centric approach tend to recall products sooner, effectively mitigating harmful incidents and yielding long-term financial benefits (Liu et al., 2017; Hoffmann et al., 2024).

5.1.2 General Product Recall Guidelines

To ensure consistent and effective recall management, organizations should develop comprehensive recall guidelines delineating procedures, responsibilities, and best practices. These guidelines should encompass critical elements such as:

- Criteria for triggering a recall, encompassing identification of safety hazards, quality defects, or regulatory non-compliance.
- Steps for evaluating the extent and seriousness of the recall, incorporating risk assessment and categorization.
- Protocols for engaging stakeholders, including customers, regulators, and the media.
- Procedures for product retrieval, replacement, or disposal, covering logistics, remedial options, process oversight, and documentation.
- Mandates for post-recall analysis, incorporating root cause inquiry and corrective measures.

The task force advocates for the creation of standardized procedures to address any potential product-harm crisis and recall scenario. These procedures should be consolidated into a comprehensive and regularly updated "how-to handbook" for easy access. By adopting such a handbook, organizations can ensure prompt, efficient, and compliant management of recall incidents in accordance with regulatory mandates and stakeholder expectations.

Organizations need not develop recall handbooks from scratch if they do not already have them. Regulatory agencies like the CPSC in the USA routinely publish and update guidelines to assist companies in crafting their own recall handbooks.[2] Additionally, the International Organization for Standardization (ISO), an independent body setting voluntary international standards, has formulated ISO 10377 to offer practical guidance on guaranteeing consumer product safety during manufacturing.[3] This standard complements ISO 10393, which delineates procedures, including a product recall program, for addressing unsafe or non-compliant consumer products once they are in the market.[4] Furthermore, ISO provides various industry- and product-specific guidelines, akin to numerous other agencies and institutions specialized in diverse sectors. For instance, GMP+, a provider of a feed safety certification scheme covering the entire feed chain, offers a guideline for executing successful recalls within the feed industry.[5] These resources furnish detailed insights on identifying and structuring various facets of product safety issues and the product recall process.

5.1.3 Training and Education Programs

Efficient recall management necessitates a proficient and knowledgeable workforce capable of promptly and effectively addressing recall incidents. Organizations should prioritize comprehensive training and educational initiatives to ensure that employees across all hierarchies and departments possess the requisite skills and understanding. These programs should encompass:

- Identification of potential recall triggers, encompassing safety hazards, quality defects, and regulatory infringements.
- Protocols for reporting and escalating potential recall concerns to the relevant authorities.

---

[2] URL: cpsc.gov/s3fs-public/CPSCRecallHandbookSeptember2021.pdf.
[3] URL: iso.org/obp/ui/#iso:std:iso:10377.
[4] URL: iso.org/obp/ui/#iso:std:iso:10393.
[5] URL: gmpplus.org/media/24opjnhi/s-9-9-executing-a-successful-recall.pdf.

- Roles and duties during recall incidents, including active involvement in recall task force operations.
- Communication guidelines for both internal and external stakeholders, encompassing media and regulatory bodies.
- Optimal practices for product retrieval, replacement, and disposal, incorporating thorough documentation and record keeping.

Various specialized agencies offer onsite and virtual recall readiness workshops and training sessions, often tailored to specific industries. Regulatory bodies also provide diverse training resources and supportive materials, such as videos and posters, designed to enhance awareness of product safety issues among frontline employees in the workplace (see Fig. 5.2). By allocating resources to continual training, education, and ongoing awareness initiatives, organizations can enhance their preparedness to effectively address recall incidents, mitigate potential risks, and safeguard both customers and their brand reputation.

5.1.4 Mock Recall Exercises

Mock recall exercises serve as key instruments for validating and refining recall procedures and protocols within a controlled setting. These exercises emulate real-world recall scenarios, enabling organizations to evaluate the efficacy of their recall plans, pinpoint any deficiencies, and enhance procedures as necessary. Typical elements of mock recall exercises encompass:

- Scenario development: Crafting authentic recall scenarios reflective of potential risks and hazards associated with the organization's products.
- Stakeholder involvement: Engaging key personnel from various departments in the exercise, including members of the recall task force, pertinent operational teams, and C-suite management.
- Implementation and assessment: Executing the mock recall exercise in line with predefined objectives and criteria, followed by a comprehensive debriefing and evaluation of performance.

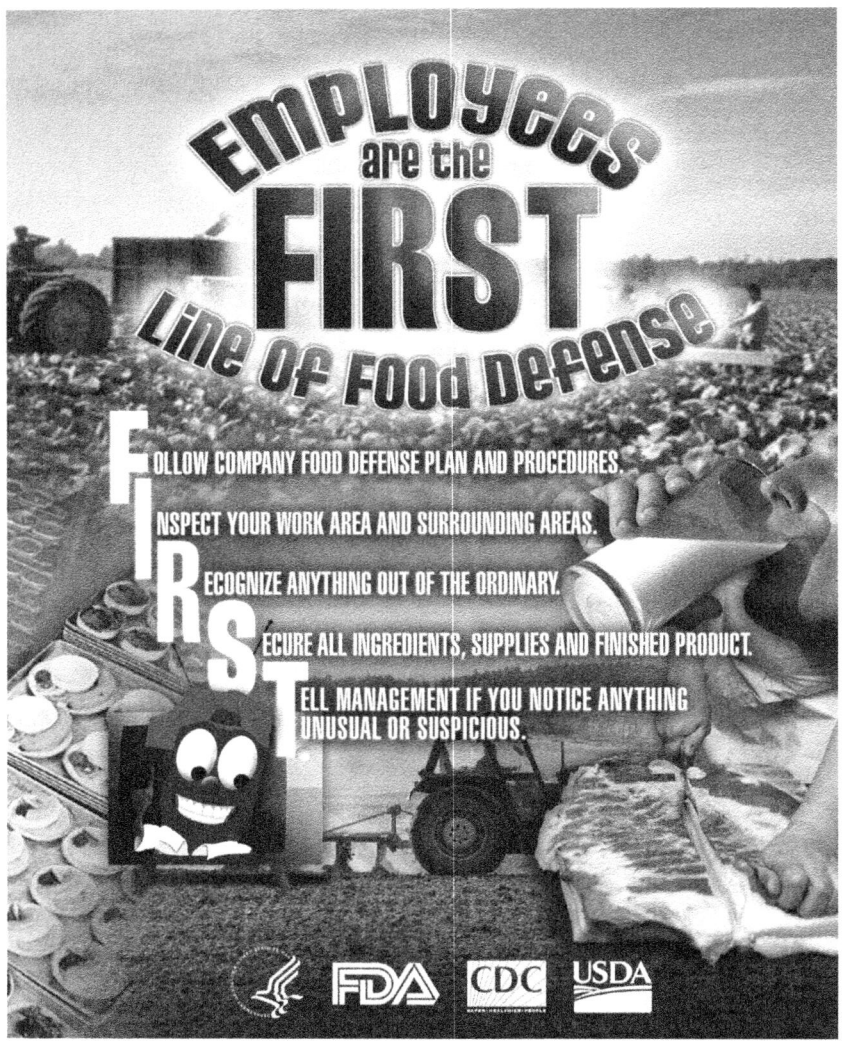

Fig. 5.2 Employees FIRST poster provided by the U.S. Food & Drug Administration. Source: FDA (2024)

- Continuous enhancement: Utilizing insights garnered from mock recall exercises to refine and bolster recall procedures, communication protocols, and training initiatives.

Regularly conducting mock recall exercises enables organizations to fortify their readiness for recall incidents, identify and rectify potential vulnerabilities, and augment overall response capabilities. For instance, in the context of the one step back and one step forward mechanism, essential for food business operators to trace both received and distributed foods, companies like Campbell's, an American food company, annually test their traceability systems (Cartwright & Healy, 2023).

> **Campbell's Traceability Program**
> Campbell's company conducts annual tests on its supply chain partners to evaluate their traceability programs, ensuring the effective tracing of materials through Supply Base Partners (SBPs) both forward and backward during mock recall exercises. SBPs are required to deploy a traceability system capable of monitoring information pertinent to Food Safety and Quality across their supply chain. This system enables the tracking of materials and services from suppliers through manufacturing to Campbell's facilities at any given juncture (Campbells, 2021).

Furthermore, the adoption of downstream traceability systems facilitates the tracing of food product origins, monitoring of food handling and processing, and tracking of product distribution. This, in turn, promotes transparency and accountability throughout the supply chain, ultimately bolstering consumer trust (Cartwright & Healy, 2023). A notable exemplar is Tyson, a prominent American food company, with approximately 81% of its facilities currently equipped with certified systems. Tyson's annual report underscores its ongoing dedication to extending these investments across all facilities, aligning with its commitment to enhancing consumer confidence, food safety, and Corporate Social Responsibility (CSR) (Hall & Johnson-Hall 2021).

5.1.5 Product Tracing, Safety, and Quality Control

Prevention is indeed preferable to remedy, especially concerning product recalls. Organizations should institute robust product tracing, safety, and quality control measures to pre-emptively identify and address potential risks before they escalate into recall situations. Research indicates that investing in downstream traceability not only demonstrates social responsibility but also yields several financial benefits. These include mitigating the impact of unsafe products during recalls, reducing the costs associated with recall execution, enhancing Corporate Social Responsibility (CSR) perception for the recalling entity, expediting accurate and timely recalls, and ultimately diminishing overall costs and risks (Maloni & Brown, 2006; Mejia et al., 2010; León-Bravo et al., 2019).

Key strategies encompass:

– Supply chain transparency: Ensuring visibility and traceability throughout the entire supply chain, from raw materials to finished products, and extending to the distribution network down to the end customer. This transparency aids in identifying potential sources of contamination or defects and facilitates the swift location of recalled products during a recall event.
– Quality assurance protocols: Implementing rigorous quality control measures at every phase of the product development and production process, encompassing raw material inspection, manufacturing processes, and finished product testing.
– Regulatory compliance: Staying abreast of pertinent regulatory requirements and industry standards, and ensuring complete compliance to mitigate the risk of non-compliance-related recalls.
– Continuous improvement: Regularly evaluating and enhancing safety and quality control procedures based on feedback, data analysis, and emerging trends or technologies.

While industries like food, pharmaceuticals, and aviation have elaborate traceability, product safety, and quality control measures due to stringent regulatory demands, instances like the Boeing 737 Max case underscore the vulnerabilities of monitoring and quality assurance systems. This example highlights challenges such as insufficient incentives for disclosure, technical complexities, limited agency resources, and political influence, which can compromise monitoring and safety protocols. Despite Boeing's longstanding reputation for safety and innovation, prioritizing cost-cutting over quality standards resulted in severe consequences during the 737 Max crisis (Isidore, 2024). This crisis has repercussions extending to airlines, previously loyal customers of Boeing, now facing blame from passengers, employees, and the public alike (Hawkins, 2024).

Emphasizing product safety monitoring and quality control measures enables organizations to mitigate recall incidents, protect consumers, and uphold their brand's reputation and integrity in the long run. Effective product recall management necessitates a comprehensive and proactive approach encompassing cross-departmental task forces, recall guidelines development, training programs implementation, mock recall exercises, and enhancement of product tracing, safety, and quality control measures. By investing in proactive measures to prevent recalls and mitigate risks, organizations can preserve consumer trust, safeguard brand reputation, and minimize the potential impact on both customers and the business.

5.2 Recall Phase: Process and Communication

In the event of product recalls, meticulous planning and swift response are imperative. The product recall process entails activities directed at pinpointing the root cause of the issue, engaging with intermediaries and end consumers, and instituting measures to avert potential future crises. Table 5.2 provides a comprehensive outline of the recall process and delineates considerations for each stage. Subsequent Sects. 5.2.1–5.2.7 offer detailed explanations of each step.

Table 5.2 Recall phase activities

Recall phase area	Activities
Problem identification	**External sources** – Third party test results – Beta testing – Gamma testing – Monitoring social media – Customer helpline **Internal sources** – Alpha testing – Quality control reports – Delta testing – Interviews with employees
Risk assessment	– Products risk – Financial risk – Liability risk
Decision on recall	– Early recalls: Costly and attract unwarranted accusations – Delayed recalls: Health risks and tarnished brand image
Recall plan creation	– Understand industry-specific standards – Define realistic goals – Determine remedy choices – Outline announcement details – Decide on communication strategies – Integrate plan with management information systems
Communication with relevant stakeholders	**Customers** – Be transparent – Provide guidelines and updates – Set up a customer service hotline or email contact – Develop a social media strategy – Update advertising campaigns – Choose a spokesperson **Wholesalers and retailers** – Send recall notifications **Public policy makers and regulators** – Notify them about problem – Provide regular updates on recall's progress **Investors and financial analysts** – Notify them about problem – Provide regular updates on recall's progress

(continued)

Table 5.2 (continued)

Recall phase area	Activities
Recall execution and monitoring	– Isolate defective products – Monitor recall effectiveness – Provide supply replacements or compensations to retailers
Documentation and reporting	– Product records – Consumer complaints – Information from suppliers – Decision-making process – Corrective actions – Recall progress – Recall effectiveness report – Disposition of recalled products

Source: Own illustration

5.2.1 Problem Identification

The capability and swiftness of a firm in identifying and addressing potential issues significantly influence the size and repercussions of a recall. While each recall scenario differs, firms typically detect problems through a combination of external and internal information sources.

External sources encompass:

- Third-party test results from regulatory agencies and organizations, such as Stiftung Warentest, a prominent European product testing organization headquartered in Germany.
- Beta testing, where real users assess the product in real-world conditions, providing direct feedback.
- Gamma testing, which involves evaluating a product's safety by other external stakeholders like distributors, media outlets, and interest groups.
- Monitoring various social media platforms and overseeing customer helplines.
- Reports from suppliers.

User feedback regarding product experiences can serve as crucial early indicators of potential product issues. However, effectively monitoring user-generated content, particularly on social media, in real time presents a challenge. It necessitates distinguishing meaningful signals from background noise to prevent either overreactions or underreactions (Mukherjee & Sinha, 2018). Employing advanced natural language processing and prediction models can aid in overcoming this challenge, ensuring unbiased decision-making.

Several internal sources also prove beneficial, including routine product testing methods like quality control, delta testing, and alpha testing. Delta testing involves periodically retrieving random product samples for performance analysis. In some cases, manufacturers can conduct comprehensive testing of all their products in use regularly. For example, airlines are legally mandated to conduct routine inspections of their aircraft after reaching specific mileage thresholds. Alpha testing, a form of acceptance testing, aims to uncover potential issues and bugs *before* the final product release to end users. This process involves internal employees of the organization conducting the testing. Additionally, interviewing employees engaged in the production or distribution of the product can yield valuable insights (Allianz, 2017; Faster Capital, 2023; Smith et al., 1996).

Managers must recognize that mishandling this phase can lead to severe consequences, even if the product is ultimately not at fault. The Audi recall serves as a notable example.

> **Audi's Poor Root Cause Analysis**
> In 1986, Audi found itself under scrutiny from the Center for Auto Safety following numerous reports of unintended acceleration incidents involving their Audi 5000 models. Despite uncertainties regarding the cause—whether technical malfunctions or driver error—Audi hesitated in its response, delaying action for 3 months before announcing a recall affecting 132,000 vehicles in July 1986. Initially considering mechanical remedies, Audi ultimately opted for a gear shift lock requiring drivers to depress the brake before shifting gears.
>
> While the recall incurred an estimated cost of $25 million, the aftermath was far more detrimental. Negative media coverage, ongoing accidents, and a subsequent class action lawsuit inflicted severe damage on the brand's reputation and sales. A study conducted by Sullivan (1990) revealed an 11.5% higher depreciation in the resale value of Audi 5000 models due to the recall, with adverse publicity also impacting the resale values of other Audi models.
>
> Despite later investigations attributing the acceleration issue primarily to driver error, the harm had already been inflicted. Sales plummeted from 74,000 units in 1985 to just over 21,000 in 1989, signaling a prolonged journey for the company to rebuild its image and regain consumer trust.

5.2.2 Risk Assessment

This process step entails a comprehensive analysis of product risks, encompassing examination of both non-financial and financial outcomes, as well as evaluation of legal liabilities (see Chap. 3 for further details). Analyzing product risk involves consideration of various factors, including:

- The scope of affected products.
- The type of hazard and its occurrence, distinguishing between normal use and misuse.
- Defect rate, indicating the likelihood of defective products (higher sales volume or defect rates can elevate risks).
- Failure rate, assessing the proportion of defective products likely to *cause injury*.
- Probability of harm to users, weighing also the severity of potential injuries (fatal or long-term injuries pose greater risks than those necessitating basic first aid).
- Market coverage extent, such as national versus regional distribution.

Financial impact encompasses costs associated with the recall, lost sales, and reputational damage to the firm. Additionally, firms must gauge potential liability exposure. While delaying a recall may result in a larger-scale problem, initiating a recall acknowledges the existence of an issue and potentially invites a wave of lawsuits (Jackson & Morgan, 1988). By conducting a thorough assessment of risk impacts, firms can prioritize their response and allocate resources effectively.

5.2.3 Decision on Recall

Firms must recognize the critical importance of promptly reaching a decision regarding a recall (Smith et al., 1996). In cases where a recall is deemed necessary, the firm must be prepared to respond swiftly, effectively, and efficiently. Acting promptly aids in mitigating allegations that the firm neglected to acknowledge the severity of the issue until a significant incident occurred (Jackson & Morgan, 1988).

There are instances where the potential harm to customers stems from an unsubstantiated accusation. Even though customers may not be at risk, ignoring such accusations could lead to significant reputational damage due to media frenzy. A notable example is the bizarre situation faced by Pepsi-Cola, which encountered a fabricated product-harm crisis.

> **Pepsi-Cola's Effective Handling of a Fake Product-Harm Crisis**
> In 1993, Pepsi-Cola faced a potential recall following reports of syringes allegedly discovered in its canned cola beverages. The saga began on Thursday, June 10, when an elderly couple from Tacoma found a syringe inside a can of Diet Pepsi. Their immediate action was to contact their lawyer, who promptly alerted the media, local health authorities, and the police.
>
> The next day, another incident unfolded when a woman in Federal Way reported a similar finding. Both incidents implicated a company bottler in Washington State, prompting the U.S. Food and Drug Administration (FDA) to caution consumers in the Pacific Northwest to pour their soda into a glass before consumption. Pepsi swiftly made executives from its local bottler, Alpac Corporation, available to the media.
>
> Despite these developments, the FDA refrained from issuing a recall, citing the absence of injuries or evidence indicating harmful substances in the syringes. Although Pepsi considered a voluntary recall, they ultimately decided against it based on the FDA's guidance that it was unnecessary due to the lack of health risk.
>
> However, reports flooded Pepsi headquarters from media outlets nationwide. In response, they quickly assembled a crisis management team comprising 12 company executives. By the following Tuesday, the company president was actively engaging with TV newsrooms. Simultaneously, a company video news release and press release, completed with graphics, were distributed to clarify the production process and emphasize the implausibility of foreign object insertion. Figure 5.3 provides a link to a video that also features the Pepsi production process.
>
> Before the company president was scheduled to appear on TV on ABC's Nightline to address their belief that the media was entangled in a significant hoax, the FDA announced the first arrest on charges of filing a false report. The ensuing breakthrough came when surveillance footage from a supermarket in Aurora captured a female shopper seemingly inserting a syringe into a can of Diet Pepsi. Pepsi promptly acquired a copy of the tape and integrated it into a video news release package distributed to television stations nationwide.
>
> Pepsi's advertising agency crafted a print ad, the company's sole paid response to the crisis. The headline boldly proclaimed: "Pepsi is pleased to announce.... nothing." The ad clarified: "As America now knows, those stories about Diet Pepsi were a hoax. Hundreds of investigators have found no evidence to support a single claim." The ad concluded with gratitude toward "the millions of you who have stood with us." It appeared in prominent newspapers like *USA Today*, *The New York Times*, and approximately a dozen other major publications the following Monday, signaling the effective resolution of the crisis (Holmes, 1993).

Fig. 5.3 Pepsi production process. Source: Snapshot from YouTube video (youtube.com/watch?v=wi9xDElHuWA)

In contrast, delaying recalls can have severe outcomes for both companies and customers, as seen in the Fisher sleepers' recall.

Fisher-Price Rock 'n Play sleepers' Slow Recall
The Fisher-Price Rock 'n Play sleeper, intended for infants, posed a significant Pepsi's fake product-harm crisis 1993 suffocation risk due to its 30-degree incline. This safety concern led to recalls and legislative actions.

In April 2019, Fisher-Price recalled nearly 4.7 million Rock 'n Play Sleepers following reports of over 30 infant deaths since its introduction to the market in 2009. Despite the alarming number of incidents, the company took a decade to initiate the recall. The recall encompassed all models of the product, despite being marketed for "all-night" sleeping, contrary to American Academy of Pediatrics safe sleep guidelines.

In January 2023, Fisher-Price reannounced the recall after at least 70 more deaths linked to the Rock 'n Play, with eight deaths occurring post the initial recall announcement. Shortly after Fisher-Price's recall, another company named Kids II recalled 694,000 rocking sleepers sold at major nationwide retailers like Walmart and Target, following at least five infant deaths associated with the Kids II Rocking Sleepers.

The reannouncement of the recall 4 years later highlights the inadequacy of the initial recall, attributed to the firm's insufficient outreach and

> incentives for participation. Consumers who purchased the product were only eligible to receive vouchers for Fisher-Price toys, which represented a fraction of the sleeper's original cost. This approach drew criticism for prioritizing profits over safety (Keller & Borwick, 2023).
>
> Figure 5.4 provides a link to the Consumer Reports documentary on this product-harm crisis.

5.2.4 Recall Plan Creation

When developing a plan, managers should consider several important factors including industry regulations, aims, remedy options, recall announcement content, communication strategies, and management information systems. Understanding these elements is crucial for effective recall management.

Firstly, managers need a comprehensive understanding of industry regulations. Regulators define specific requirements for firms, such as providing details about faulty products, identifying distributors and

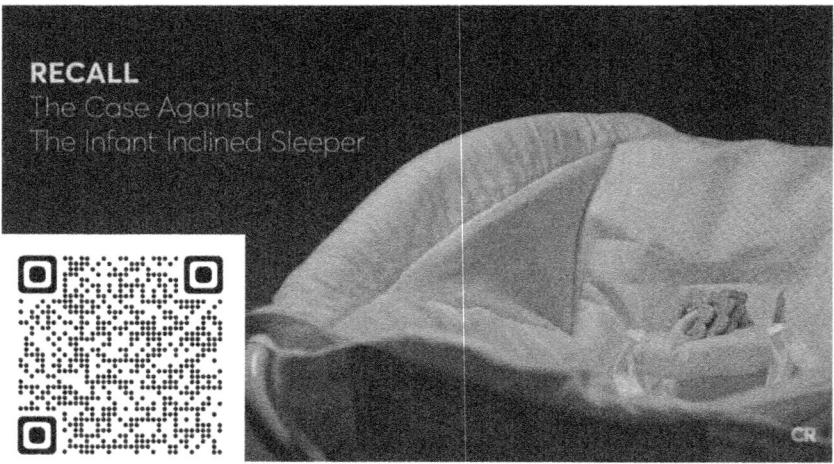

Fig. 5.4 Fisher-Price Rock 'n Play recall documentary by Consumer Reports. Source: Snapshot from YouTube video (youtube.com/watch?v=NdDCbqZxJ3w)

affected customers, and developing a strategy for either disposing of or correcting the product. It is crucial to know these requirements to prepare an effective plan (Faster Capital, 2023).

Secondly, managers should define clear and achievable targets, taking into account factors such as the product type, its age, and associated risks. For example, ensuring a specific percentage of distributed products are returned (Smith et al., 1996).

In the third step, managers should determine the extent of the required response and the appropriate remedy. There are several remedies that can be offered, including:

– Repairing the product to eliminate the hazard.
– Replacing the product with a hazard-free alternative.
– Providing a full refund upon return.
– Issuing warning labels or updated usage instructions for safe handling.
– Implementing a software patch or update.

It is important for companies to prioritize simplicity in the recall process. They should aim to reduce complexity by minimizing the steps required for consumers to obtain a repair, replacement, or refund. For instance, companies could request consumers to return the product to the original place of purchase or to a designated repair center. In the case of large products, arranging a courier service to collect the item could be beneficial. Additionally, providing options like sending a technician for on-site repair or handling the removal and repair of the product, including any property damage, can enhance convenience for customers (ACCC, 2023).

Companies may request proof of purchase from consumers to verify that the affected product was indeed supplied by them. However, consumers may not always need to present a receipt to qualify for a remedy. They might have received the product as a gift or bought it a long time ago. Proof of ownership could include various forms such as a receipt, bank statement, returning part or all of the product, warranty registration information, a photo of the product in their possession, or details from a loyalty program (ACCC, 2023).

Next, firms should decide on communication strategies, channels, and formats. Firms should use multiple communication channels to ensure reaching as many customers as possible. This includes press releases, social media, email, and direct mail. Furthermore, for urgent recalls, firms must consider utilizing phone calls or text messages (Faster Capital, 2023). The choice of communication format, either visual or textual, also impacts the effectiveness of recall warnings. Research shows that imagery proves more effective than textual information in alerting consumers to product recalls (Trendel et al., 2018).

The recalling firm should additionally define the announcement details (including who will make it, when and where, who needs to be notified, and the script content) and organize the field response program (clarifying who will handle the acceptance of faulty products, outlining the company's strategy for monitoring returned products and specifying the entity responsible for providing repairs or replacements).

Many firms already have crisis-management communications plans designed to handle various crises, such as labor relations problems or regulatory investigations. Recalls should be included in such plans. For firms that are designing crisis-management communication plans, a recall scenario could be an appropriate prototype issue.

Lastly, the integration of recall planning into management information systems databases is also essential for logistics. This integration ensures the retention of product traceability records linked to customer files and enables the firm to keep track of the recall's progress. The capability to monitor product ownership via customer files is valuable in ensuring that accurate information, including flaws and remedies, is being effectively communicated and implemented. Furthermore, it helps managers evaluate recall effectiveness and reach out to distributors, retailers, and customers who have not responded to the recall (Smith et al., 1996).

It is crucial to emphasize that executing all the outlined steps during a product-harm crisis, especially when the firm is on the brink of initiating a product recall, is impractical. As delineated in Sect. 5.1, firms must be prepared for recalls in advance. The "How-to" handbook (refer Sect. 5.1.2) ought to encompass all the aforementioned aspects, ideally tailored to the specifics of the ongoing recall scenario. As the recall is being prepared and executed, only minimal adjustments to the overarching guidelines should suffice.

5.2.5 Communication with Relevant Stakeholders

The key step includes effective communication with stakeholders, especially customers and distributors (see Chap. 4) because without their swift response, effective recall management is not possible. But managers overseeing recalls should also identify other stakeholders in the recall process, extending beyond customers and distributors. These might include public policymakers and regulators, the media, and financial market actors. Clearly, it is crucial to build the firm's credibility in the eyes of these stakeholders via effective communication.

Customers represent the most crucial stakeholder groups. Key factors during communication with customers include transparency and easy-to-understand statements about recommended actions. Customers need to be informed about the specifics of the recall, such as:

- Description of the product: This includes name, model, batch or serial numbers, and production date.
- High resolution images of the product.
- How or why the problem happened: It is important to avoid technical language while explaining the problem.
- Potential harm of the product: Describe the associated risk and guide consumers on how to identify the problem.
- Remedy offered.
- Easy-to-understand and non-technical instructions on follow-up steps (e.g., guidelines on product return procedures, acquiring refunds or replacements).
- Injury or death reports (as this underscores the urgency of action); however, statements like "no incidents have occurred" could downplay the potential risk and should be avoided
- Contact information.

When designing the recall message, managers should incorporate call-to-action statements. For instance, "Remove [product] from your child's toy box and return it to us for a replacement [product]." Firms should refrain from employing language in any communication that downplays the risk to consumers, such as "precautionary," "low risk," and "secondary impact" (ACCC, 2023). The frequently used term "voluntary recall" is counterproductive and misleading because it also signals that *participation* in the recall is voluntary. Furthermore, the regulatory agency overseeing the recall provides detailed communication guidelines. They cover everything from mandatory media notifications to language requirements, such as detailing symptoms of foodborne illness in recall materials. Familiarizing with these guidelines is crucial for any company when crafting recall notices (Mitchell, 2012). The illustration provided in Fig. 5.5 demonstrates a model recall advertisement design along with essential information that should be incorporated.

Additionally, firms should establish a customer service hotline or email address for customers to reach out with any questions or concerns. For example, during the Galaxy Note 7 battery issues, discussed in Chap. 1, Samsung provided a customer hotline and explained the problem and corrective actions. This approach ensured customers felt informed and heard. Firms should also communicate delays and inform customers when the products are deemed safe again. A good example is Chipotle. In 2015, Chipotle, an American restaurant chain, experienced an *E. coli* outbreak. During the recall, the firm kept customers updated about the safety measures they were taking and communicated reopening delays. This helped the firm to maintain customer trust (Faster Capital, 2023).

The next crucial factor is having a carefully planned social media strategy for effective management of a product recall in the media. A well-planned social media strategy enables a brand to communicate with customers, alleviate their concerns, and handle the crisis. For instance, social media listening tools can be helpful during a product recall. These tools enable companies to actively monitor social media platforms for any mentions related to the brand and the recall itself. By keeping a close eye on social media, companies can promptly address customer inquiries, concerns, and address any misinformation circulating. Additionally, social media listening tools aid in tracking sentiment and assessing the overall mood of customers, facilitating a more informed response strategy (Faster Capital, 2023).

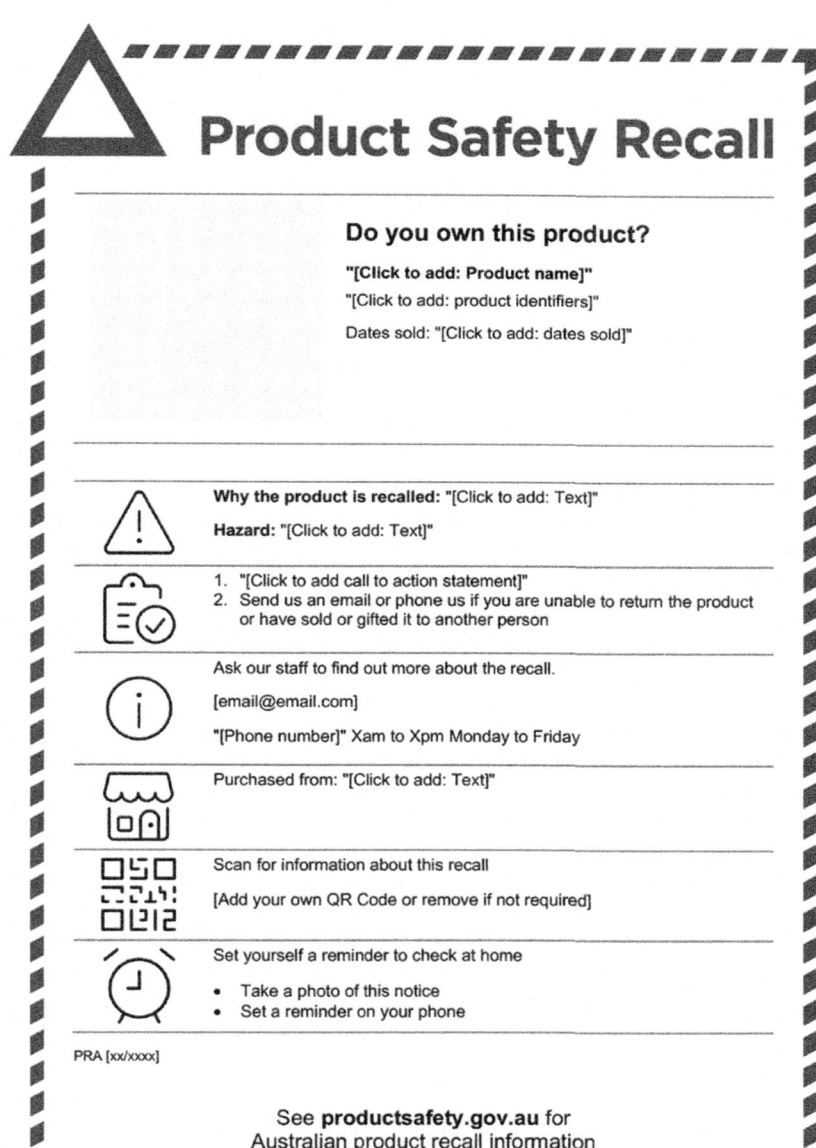

Fig. 5.5 Recall advertisement template of the Australian Competition & Consumer Commission. Note: Frame, warning triangle, and title in signal red in the original template. Source: ACCC (2024; URL: productsafety.gov.au/recalls/conducting-a-consumer-product-safety-recall/tell-the-accc-of-the-recall)

Moreover, companies can utilize other options such as paid social media ads and pinned posts on the company's social media pages. Utilizing paid options on social media platforms, such as boosting posts, can increase views and extend the reach of the recall message beyond immediate followers. It is likely that only a few customers are actively following the brand on social media. Paid advertising can effectively target those who received the product as a gift or purchased it second-hand (ACCC, 2023). It is also recommended to:

- Ask followers to share and tag friends or family members who might be impacted by the recall.
- Engage with comments on the recall post.
- Express gratitude for shares/tags.
- Address any inquiries about the recall.
- Ensure sufficient staff are available, particularly in the initial days after the recall announcement, when many consumers may have questions or need additional details.
- Repost the recall message multiple times throughout the recall period to reach more customers.

However, since social media posts have limited space to convey all essential information, it is advisable to provide a link directing consumers to the recall advertisement posted on the company's or regulator's website. To accomplish this, companies can create a dedicated product safety recall page on their website, ensuring it includes all the necessary information. It should be optimized to display effectively on mobile devices (ACCC, 2023).

Simultaneously, marketers should review existing communication campaigns to ensure that scheduled advertisements do not encourage uninformed consumers to buy or use recalled items. The firm might also need to revise its promotional strategy. For instance, they could precede their existing advertising with recall campaigns, using online advertising. It is essential to determine the timing, frequency, and duration of the advertising efforts.

However, to maintain message consistency across various communication channels, firms can utilize a spokesperson. The spokesperson should be knowledgeable about the recall and able to respond to inquiries from stakeholders and the media. Research indicates that the choice of spokesperson delivering the message, whether it's the CEO or another representative, also influences consumer reactions to product recalls (Wang & Wang, 2014). In particular, consumers characterized by high levels of power distance are less likely to decrease their purchase intention when the firm employs a CEO as the spokesperson (Laufer et al., 2018).

A prime example is Mattel's recall, which is also described in Chap. 1. In August 2007, Mattel recalled millions of toys due to lead contamination. During the recall, the company and CEO were publicly visible and available. For instance, on the day of the recall, Robert Eckert, Mattel's CEO, met with reporters and engaged in television and phone interviews. The CEO also issued a public apology (Bartz, 2007). Thus, in cases of high recall severity, a company representative, such as CEO, should explain the issues and talk to internal and external stakeholders.

While offering an apologetic response to a faulty product is a reasonable approach, the manner in which the apology is crafted holds significant importance (Antonetti & Baghi, 2023). A company may acknowledge that its capabilities were insufficient in preventing product failure but express a commitment to implementing substantial improvements in both processes and product quality moving forward. However, if the company has a history of product recalls, questions regarding its competence arise, or if the product failure directly impacts its core business without external justifications (such as supplier issues), admitting inadequacy in skills to avert the recall may not be prudent. In such cases, emphasizing sincere efforts to enhance processes and product quality in the future becomes less convincing.

Managers should also consider the brand's warmth, defined as the degree to which a brand can demonstrate caring and evoke emotions and empathy within the market. Warmth is associated with friendliness, trustworthiness, and sincerity. Research indicates that perceived brand warmth influences customers in two significant ways (Astvansh et al., 2024). Customers who perceive a brand as warm are more inclined to provide "friendly" feedback to firms rather than lodging "aggressive" complaints about product failures and incidents of harm. This feedback can aid in the early detection of product failures (see Sect. 5.2.1).

Moreover, it is essential to address this aspect in recovery messages. Acknowledging the customer's feedback motive enhances customer satisfaction.

Retailers should be informed of recall information to facilitate clarification for consumers seeking it. Additionally, distributors must be notified simultaneously with the initial announcement to secure early cooperation from intermediaries. This approach helps prevent customer confusion, such as seeking refunds or repairs from dealers before they have been informed of their role in the process. In response, retailers must collaborate closely with manufacturers to ensure effective communication during a product recall. This collaboration involves sharing customer contact information, coordinating recall efforts, and aligning messaging to prevent customer confusion. Establishing a strong partnership with manufacturers allows retailers to streamline the recall process and ensure that accurate and consistent information reaches customers (Smith et al., 1996; Faster Capital, 2023).

Consistent and clear communication with regulatory agencies and legal teams is also crucial during the recall. This involves informing them of the issue and regularly updating them on the recall's progress. Poor communication can result in delays and potentially incur significant costs for the recalling firm. However, better collaboration not only saves time but also enhances information sharing, thereby reducing the burden on recalling firms to provide identical records to multiple agencies. Legal teams will also play a vital role in assessing the company's liability and ensuring compliance with all legal requirements during the recall process. This involves addressing any potential legal claims that may emerge. When coordinating with regulatory agencies and legal teams during a product recall, companies have various options to consider. Some may prefer handling the process internally, while others might opt to collaborate with third-party experts to ensure compliance with all requirements. The optimal choice will ultimately depend on the unique circumstances of the recall and the resources at the company's disposal. For instance, a small company may lack the resources required to manage a large-scale product recall internally and may need to engage outside experts. Conversely, a larger company with an established legal team might be more adept at handling the process internally (Faster Capital, 2023).

Finally, managers are advised to use the media as a means of delivering the recall message. This can be divided into news websites with national, regional, and local reach. Traditionally, recall notices are placed on national news websites due to their extensive reach and wide audience base. Nevertheless, by using statistical and lifestyle survey data from sources like Nielsen Scarborough and The Alliance for Audited Media (AAM), managers can pinpoint websites and publications that are more prone to being read by owners of a specific type of product. Furthermore, creating educational content is considered a proactive approach in digital media management. This content could include explainer videos (as shown in Pepsi's recall case in Sect. 5.2.3), infographics, and blog posts that explain the reasons behind the recall and outline the steps being taken to rectify the issue (Faster Capital, 2024).

5.2.6 Recall Execution and Monitoring

During this stage, managers need to take into account three crucial elements: isolating returned items, overseeing the recall effectiveness, and implementing remedies.

Firstly, returned products should be separated from other items to prevent defective products from being unintentionally shipped out again. This requires effective logistics and information systems to trace any product they have handled or processed. Systems should isolate defective items by batch, plant, process, or shift, using identifiers like serial numbers. This aids in monitoring the progress of recalls and documenting recall effectiveness.

Next, as previously emphasized in Chap. 3, another critical aspect of recall management is recall effectiveness. Managers must set a recall effectiveness rate and maintain oversight and control over the recall's outcomes. This enables them to evaluate the efficiency of the recall message delivery. Two primary dimensions of recall effectiveness are:

- *Recall compliance rate*: The percentage of recalled products that are remedied, which can include being repaired, returned, replaced, deactivated, or disposed of.

– *Recall completion speed*: The difference between the recall completion date and the recall announcement date.

In most countries, the prioritization for recall monitoring hinges on the risk level associated with a product, considering both the severity and immediacy of the potential danger to human health or safety. Other factors, such as the product's lifespan or price, are also taken into consideration and carefully weighed. For example, while a lower recall effectiveness may be suitable for inexpensive, low-risk items sold several years ago, opting for a higher recall effectiveness rate would be wise for expensive products with a higher perceived risk. If a recall is deemed ineffective and unsafe products persist on the market, or if a company continues to receive incident reports related to a recalled product, authorities may invite or request the company to extend, revise, or enhance its recall strategy to improve effectiveness. Thus, it is imperative for businesses to establish systems for closely monitoring recall effectiveness. This not only safeguards public health and safety but also helps prevent the additional costs associated with extending or revising a recall (OECD, 2018).

Implementing the remedy offer requires cooperation from the distribution network. If the product is to be returned to retailers, these intermediaries must agree to manage the returns and any compensation that will be provided to consumers. If dealers have to repair the defective product, a sufficient supply of replacement parts must be made readily available to them (Smith et al., 1996).

5.2.7 Documentation and Reporting

During the recall, it is imperative to record all steps for legal and internal purposes and report to regulatory authorities. Documenting information during the recall enables an efficient audit of the procedures, aiding managers in tracking recall effectiveness, identifying weaknesses and strengths, conducting more precise quality and performance tests on new products, and foreseeing potential future recalls. This includes:

- Product records (e.g., technical files, quality defect investigations, test certificates, and distribution locations)
- Customer complaints
- Information from suppliers (e.g., retests)
- Decision-making process
- Corrective actions
- Progress of the recall process
- Recall effectiveness report
- Formal disposition of all recalled batches.

This documentation not only ensures compliance with legal requirements but also serves as a crucial basis for initiating structured learning processes in the post-recall phase (European Commission, 2016).

5.3 Post-Recall Phase: Recovery and Learning

A product recall can be a major challenge for any company, affecting not only its bottom line but also its reputation and customer trust. When a recall happens, it can lead to significant damage to the brand, undermine customer confidence, and reduce overall satisfaction with the affected products. Additionally, there is the risk of legal repercussions due to safety concerns, which can further impact the company's financial health.

While it is essential to prepare for and execute a recall effectively to mitigate these risks (as discussed in Sects. 5.1 and 5.2), it is unrealistic to expect to completely avoid negative outcomes. However, in this chapter, we will explore strategies that managers can use to bounce back and emerge stronger from a product-harm crisis.

After a recall, managers have several key objectives. Firstly, they need to work on restoring both non-financial performance like customer trust and corporate reputation, as well as financial performance, including regaining lost customers and maintaining existing ones, and getting revenue back to pre-crisis levels. Secondly, it is crucial to learn from the crisis to prevent similar incidents in the future and to optimize strategies to minimize damage if another recall occurs. Thorough documentation and reporting (as detailed in Sect. 5.2.7) play a vital role in this process, helping to identify areas for improvement systematically.

5.3.1 Performance Recovery

Managers faced with the challenge of restoring firm performance following a recall have a range of options to consider. Two key strategies are often debated: adjusting product prices and modifying advertising expenditures. However, determining the optimal direction for these adjustments is not a simple task.

For instance, while increasing prices might safeguard short-term revenue, lowering them could facilitate the recovery of lost customers or retention of existing ones. Similarly, ramping up advertising spending may help to win back lost customers, but cutting these costs could bolster post-crisis cash flows.

Research has delved into the effectiveness of adjustments within these marketing metrics. Typically, recalls are followed by a period where the brand's advertising effectiveness declines, and customers become more sensitive to price changes (Van Heerde et al., 2007). However, while increasing advertising by the recalling brand post-recall has shown a positive effect on the brand's share within its category, adjustments in product prices appear to be less effective (Cleeren et al., 2013).

It is essential to recognize the significant differences between product-harm crises. For example, the level of negative media coverage regarding product defects varies widely. While some recalls, like the Volkswagen Dieselgate (see case descriptions in Sects. 3.1 and 3.2), receive extensive negative media attention, others fly largely under the press's radar. Research suggests that after widely covered recalls, the decrease in advertising effectiveness is less severe. However, the extent of negative media coverage does not seem to affect the increase in price sensitivity regarding the brand's products (Cleeren et al., 2013).

Another differentiating factor is whether the recalling firm publicly accepts blame for the product defect. Some companies choose to openly admit fault when facing a product recall, while others opt to deflect blame onto others, as seen in instances like the mislabeled Vanilla Florentine

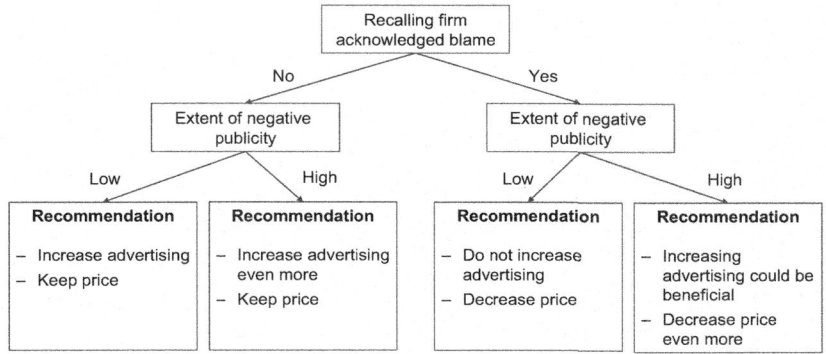

Fig. 5.6 Recommended post-recall measures based on recall characteristics. Source: Adapted from Cleeren et al. (2013)

Cookies, where seller and supplier engage in a "blame game" (see example in Sect. 4.4). Following a recall, the decrease in advertising effectiveness and the increase in price sensitivity are even more pronounced when the recalling firm publicly accepts blame for the defects (Cleeren et al., 2013).

These research findings provide practical guidance for managers. They should acknowledge the decrease in advertising effectiveness and increased price sensitivity post-recall, adjusting strategies accordingly. Effective post-recall measures will vary depending on the specific circumstances (see Fig. 5.6. If the recalling firm has not accepted blame for the defects, boosting advertising efforts may be viable, especially amid significant negative media attention. Conversely, if blame has been accepted, reducing product prices is advisable, particularly with extensive negative media coverage. In such cases, increasing advertising may also be appropriate, depending on the balance between positive media effects and the drawbacks of accepting blame.

In addition to selecting effective marketing measures post-recall, managers must also craft an appropriate communication strategy. A successful example was seen in Kraft's response after the recall of its entire peanut butter assortment in Australia in 1996 (see also case description in Sect. 3.3).

5.3.2 Learning from the Crisis

> **Kraft Peanut Butter Recall in Australia (Revisited): Selecting the Right Advertising Focus**
> In 1996, Kraft Australia faced a significant recall crisis when its peanut butter products were linked to salmonella poisoning among customers. The company had to recall all peanut butter products in Australia and suspend further distribution for over 4 months. Despite facing severe criticism and lawsuits due to its slow response, Kraft managed to recover relatively quickly from the crisis.
>
> After resolving the safety issues stemming from the recall, Kraft made a strategic decision to prioritize advertising for its flagship peanut butter brand, Kraft, over its other brand, Eta. With an investment of AU$3 million in national advertising, Kraft aimed to facilitate the relaunch of its primary peanut butter brand. This move proved successful, resulting in a swift rebound in sales for the main brand (see Fig. 5.7). Although competitor Sanitarium initially benefited from Kraft's crisis, the Australian peanut butter market soon returned to its pre-crisis conditions (Van Heerde et al., 2007).

A crucial objective in the aftermath of a product recall is to assess the recall process thoroughly to pinpoint weaknesses and implement necessary improvements. By utilizing reports, documentation, and data analytics gathered during the recall process, managers can identify areas for enhancement, reducing the likelihood of future recalls and optimizing the management of any future incidents. Research indicates that firms indeed learn from product recalls, leading to a decrease in the occurrence of future incidents (Thirumalai & Sinha, 2011). These learning effects are particularly evident following severe recalls. Studies show that an increase in recall volume (total number of recalled units) correlates with reduced

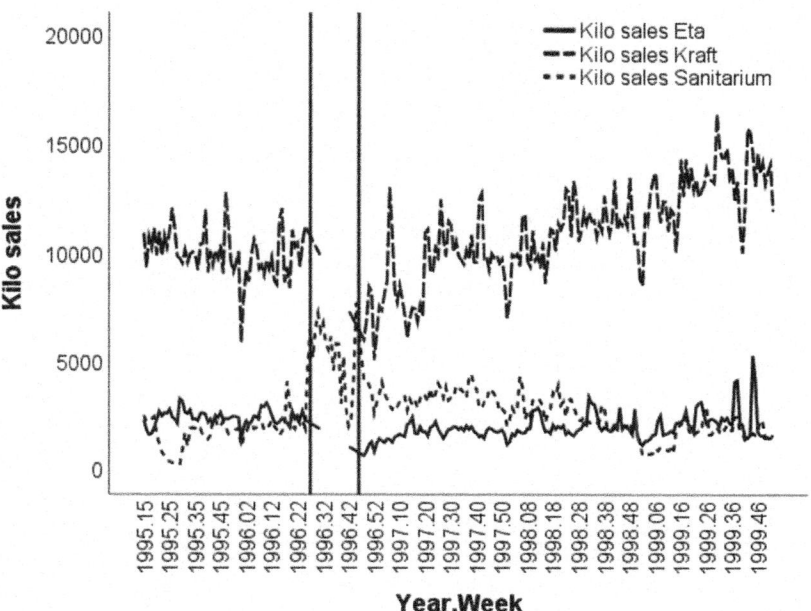

Fig. 5.7 Sales recovery of Kraft's peanut butter brands. Source: Updated from Van Heerde et al. (2007)

chances of subsequent recalls and future injuries associated with recalled products (Kalaignanam et al., 2013).

Repeated recalls signal a failure to adequately learn from past incidents. Recent research suggests that enhancements in a firm's marketing and operational capabilities can lower the likelihood of future recalls (Chakravarty et al., 2022). A notable example of a company that learned from a recall crisis and implemented improvements is General Motors (GM) (also discussed in Sect. 4.1).

> **GM's Faulty Ignition Switch Recall (Revisited): Improving Safety and Learning Culture**
>
> In 2014, GM issued a recall for 2.6 million cars due to ignition switch defects (Krisher, 2014). The flaw could lead to the engine shutting down suddenly, rendering crucial safety mechanisms such as airbags inoperative. As of 2005, at least 97 fatalities have been attributed to this issue (Plumer, 2015). Reports regarding when and how GM's senior executives became aware of the faulty switches vary. Several reports point out, however, that GM was informed about the faulty switches several years before the recall was initiated.
>
> Addressing reporters (see Fig. 5.8), Mary Barra, the CEO of GM at the time, admitted errors in the company's safety processes and expressed, "I want to start by saying how sorry personally and how sorry General Motors is for what has happened. Clearly lives have been lost and families are affected, and that is very serious" (Edmondson, 2014).
>
> This public apology marked an important first step in the development of an improved safety culture at GM. Subsequently, in March 2014, Barra announced the appointment of a new vehicle safety chief, Jeff Boyer, who was tasked with helping the company address safety issues. According to GM's announcement, the safety chief would not only be responsible for the safety development of GM vehicle systems but also oversee confirmation and validation of safety performance, along with post-sale safety activities, including recalls. Additionally, the safety chief was required to maintain regular communication with the CEO and other senior management at GM regarding vehicle safety matters. GM also launched an internal investigation to identify all errors in the company's safety processes and provide sufficient information to learn from the crisis (Edmondson, 2014).

As described in the above example, GM created a new safety-focused leadership role after the major recall in 2014. However, managers should be mindful that while establishing a new leadership role dedicated to recalls and safety signifies a serious commitment, it also poses the risk of compartmentalizing safety, which ideally should be everyone's responsibility within a company. Therefore, it is crucial to cultivate a safe environment where individuals feel empowered to engage in open and honest dialogue, especially when confronted with challenges or mistakes. Employees who point out product defects and safety issues should be welcomed rather than penalized (Edmondson, 2014).

5 The Product Recall Management Cycle   111

Fig. 5.8 The CEO of GM issues an apology amidst recall. Source: Snapshot from YouTube video (youtube.com/watch?v=LaSVVffDT2c)

In appropriate circumstances, product recalls and safety issues can serve as catalysts for change and innovation (Haunschild & Sullivan, 2002). While product recall crises demand significant resources from firms, they can also inspire managers to enhance product quality and safety through innovation. Thus, recalls have the potential to kickstart learning and innovation processes up to a certain threshold.

However, if recall frequency exceeds a certain level, firms may lack the resources to pursue innovation as they must allocate all resources to recall processes and crisis recovery. This argument is supported by researchers who have identified an inverted U-shaped relationship between recall frequency and firm innovation, particularly pronounced for firms experiencing strong growth trajectories (Ni et al., 2023).

As highlighted throughout this book, product recalls pose a significant challenge for the recalling firm, and the adverse performance implications should not be underestimated. However, recalling firms have options to expedite recovery from the crisis (see Sect. 5.3.1). Moreover, as is typical in most crisis situations, opportunities can arise from product recalls. Under the right conditions, product recalls can stimulate change and innovation within the company, reducing the likelihood of recurring safety defects and safeguarding both the firm and its customers from future adversities.

References

Allianz. (2017). *Product Recall: Managing the Impact of The New Risk Landscape*. Retrieved February 5, 2024, from https://commercial.allianz.com/content/dam/onemarketing/commercial/commercial/reports/AGCS-Product-Recall-Report.pdf.

Antonetti, P., & Baghi, I. (2023). Projecting lower competence to boost apology effectiveness: Underlying mechanism and boundary conditions. *Journal of the Academy of Marketing Science, 51*(3), 695–715.

Astvansh, V., Suri, A., & Damavandi, H. (2024). Brand warmth elicits feedback, not complaints. *Journal of the Academy of Marketing Science*, 1–23.

Australian Competition & Consumer Commission. (2023). *Supplier checklist for conducting a recall*. Retrieved March 16, 2024, from https://www.productsafety.gov.au/recalls/conducting-a-consumer-product-safety-recall/recall-tools-and-guidelines/supplier-checklist-for-conducting-a-recall.

Australian Competition & Consumer Commission (2024). *Tell the ACCC of the recall*. Retrieved May 6, 2024, from https://productsafety.gov.au/recalls/conducting-a-consumer-product-safety-recall/tell-the-accc-of-the-recall.

Bartz, D. (2007, September 12). Mattel apologizes for recalls, backs stronger CPSC. Reuters. Retrieved February 8, 2024, from https://www.reuters.com/article/idUSN12248840/.

Campbells. (2021). *Supply base requirements and expectations manual (SBREM)*. Retrieved February 8, 2024, from https://www.campbellsoupcompany.com/wp-content/uploads/2021/02/Campbell_Supply-Base-Requirements-and-Expectation-Manual-English.pdf.

Carlton, J., & Yoder, S. K. (1994, December 21). Humble pie: Intel to replace its Pentium chips. *The Wall Street Journal*, B1.

Cartwright, J. & Healy, C.(2023, April 26). From farm to fork: The vital role of traceability in meeting the UK's sustainable food demands and fighting food fraud. Charles Russell Speechlys. Retrieved February 8, 2024, from https://blog.charlesrussellspeechlys.com/post/102id5w/from-farm-to-fork-the-vital-role-of-traceability-in-meeting-the-uks-sustainable.

Chakravarty, A., Saboo, A. R., & Xiong, G. (2022). Marketing's and Operations' roles in product recall prevention: Antecedents and consequences. *Production and Operations Management, 31*(3), 1174–1190.

Cleeren, K., van Heerde, H. J., & Dekimpe, M. G. (2013). Rising from the ashes: How brands and categories can overcome product-harm crises. *Journal of Marketing, 77*(2), 58–77.

Corcoran, E. (1994, December 21). Intel to replace chips The Washington Post. Retrieved April 15, 2024, from https://www.washingtonpost.com/archive/politics/1994/12/21/intel-to-replace-chips/1ec2c929-aaa5-449a-9dbc-3db322d8d013/.

Edmondson, A. C. (2014, November 2). Fixing a weak safety culture at general motors. *Harvard Business Review*. Retrieved February 8, 2024, from https://hbr.org/2014/03/fixing-a-weak-safety-culture-at-general-motors.

European Commission. (2016). *EudraLex—volume 4-good manufacturing practice (GMP) guidelines*. Retrieved February 8, 2024, from https://health.ec.europa.eu/medicinal-products/eudralex/eudralex-volume-4_en.

Faster Capital. (2023, April 14). *Crisis management: Navigating crises: The art of handling product recalls*. Retrieved February 8, 2024, from https://fastercapital.com/content/Crisis-management%2D%2DNavigating-Crises%2D%2DThe-Art-of-Handling-Product-Recalls.html#Implementing-Corrective-Actions-and-Preventive-Measures.

Faster Capital. (2024, April 4). *Public relations: The PR nightmare: Managing product recalls in the media update*. Retrieved May 29, 2024, from https://fastercapital.com/content/Public-relations%2D%2DThe-PR-Nightmare%2D%2DManaging-Product-Recalls-in-the-Media-update.html. Accessed March 29, 2024.

Food & Drug Administration. (2024, May 3). *Food defense awareness for frontline food industry workers*. Retrieved May 3, 2024, from https://fda.gov/food/food-defense-training-education/employees-first.

Hall, D. C., & Johnson-Hall, T. D. (2021). Recall effectiveness, strategy, and task complexity in the U.S. meat and poultry industry. *International Journal of Production Economics, 234*, 1–13.

Haunschild, P. R., & Sullivan, B. N. (2002). Learning from complexity: Effects of prior accidents and incidents on airlines' learning. *Administrative Science Quarterly, 47*(4), 609–643.

Hawkins, E. (2024, January 25). Airlines blame Boeing for reputational damage. *Axios*. Retrieved April 15, 2024, from https://www.axios.com/2024/01/25/airlines-turn-on-boeing.

Hearit, K. M. (1999). Newsgroups, activist publics, and corporate apologia: The case of Intel and its Pentium chip. *Public Relations Review, 25*(3), 291–308.

Hoffmann, A. O. I., Cheong, C. S., Phan, H.-L., & Zurbruegg, R. (2024). So, sue me if you can! How legal changes diminishing managers' risk of being held liable by shareholders affect firms' likelihood to recall products. *Journal of Marketing.* https://doi.org/10.1177/00222429241231236

Holmes, P. (1993, July 6). How the Pepsi syringe hoax fizzled (1993). PRovoke media. Retrieved March 29, 2024, from https://www.provokemedia.com/latest/article/how-the-pepsi-syringe-hoax-fizzled-(1993).

Isidore, C. (2024, February 5). Boeing was once known for safety and engineering. But critics say an emphasis on profits changed that. CNN. Retrieved April 15, 2024, from https://edition.cnn.com/2024/01/30/business/boeing-history-of-problems/index.html.

Jackson, G. C., & Morgan, F. W. (1988). Responding to recall requests: A strategy for managing goods withdrawal. *Journal of Public Policy & Marketing, 7*, 152–165.

Kalaignanam, K., Kushwaha, T., & Eilert, M. (2013). The impact of product recalls on future product reliability and future accidents: Evidence from the automobile industry. *Journal of Marketing, 77*(2), 41–57. https://doi.org/10.1509/jm.11.0356

Keller, A., & Borwick, K. (2023, July 20). Fisher-price rock 'n play'. Consumer notice. Retrieved February 8, 2024, from https://www.consumernotice.org/products/child-safety/fisher-price-rock-n-play/.

Krisher, T. (2014, May 8). GM recall leaves customers frustrated and waiting. *Hendersonville Times-News.* Retrieved April 15, 2024, from https://eu.blueridgenow.com/story/news/2014/05/08/gm-recall-leaves-customers-frustrated-and-waiting/28317124007/.

Laufer, D., Garrett, T. C., & Ning, B. (2018). The moderating role of power distance on the reaction of consumers to the CEO as a spokesperson during a product harm crisis: Insights from China and South Korea. *Journal of International Management, 24*(3), 215–221.

León-Bravo, V., Caniato, F., & Caridi, M. (2019). Sustainability in multiple stages of the food supply chain in Italy: Practices, performance and reputation. *Operations Management Research, 12*(1–2), 40–61.

Lewis, P. H. (1994, December 13). I.B.M. Deals blow to a rival as it suspends pentium sales. *The New York Times.* Retrieved April 15, 2024, from https://www.nytimes.com/1994/12/13/us/ibm-deals-blow-to-a-rival-as-it-suspends-pentium-sales.html.

Liu, A. X., Liu, Y., Luo, T., & Wang, R. (2023). Impacts of chief marketing officer in product recalls. *Marketing Letters*, 1–13.

Liu, Y., Shankar, V., & Yun, W. (2017). Crisis management strategies and the long-term effects of product recalls on firm value. *Journal of Marketing, 81*(5), 30–48.

Maloni, M. J., & Brown, M. E. (2006). Corporate social responsibility in the supply chain: An application in the food industry. *Journal of Business Ethics, 68*(1), 35–52.

Mejia, C., McEntire, J., Keener, K., et al. (2010). Traceability (product tracing) in food systems: Cost considerations and implications. *Comprehensive Reviews in Food Science and Food Safety, 9*, 159–175.

Mitchell, H. (2012, June 1). Communicating during and through a food recall. *Food Safety Magazine*. Retrieved March 17, 2024, from https://www.food-safety.com/articles/3780-communicating-during-and-through-a-food-recall.

Mukherjee, U. K., & Sinha, K. K. (2018). Product recall decisions in medical device supply chains: A big data analytic approach to evaluating judgment bias. *Production and Operations Management, 27*(10), 1816–1833.

Ni, J., Borisov, A., Modi, S., & Huang, X. (2023). Learning from failure: The implications of product recalls for firm innovation. *Journal of Supply Chain Management, 59*(3), 42–64.

OECD. (2018). *Enhancing product recall effectiveness globally: OECD background report*. OECD Science, Technology and Industry Policy Papers, No. 58, OECD Publishing, Paris. https://doi.org/10.1787/ef71935c-en.

Plumer, B. (2015 May 11). The GM recall scandal of 2014. Vox. Retrieved April 15, 2024, from https://www.vox.com/2014/10/3/18073458/gm-car-recall.

Ramirez, A. (1994, December 13). Stocks gain despite Intel's Chip problem. *The New York Times*. Retrieved April 15, 2024, from https://www.nytimes.com/1994/12/13/business/stocks-gain-despite-intel-s-chip-problem.html.

Smith, N. C., Thomas, R. J., & Quelch, J. (1996). A strategic approach to managing product recalls. *Harvard Business Review*. Retrieved February 8, 2024, from https://hbr.org/1996/09/a-strategic-approach-to-managing-product-recalls.

Sullivan, M. (1990). Measuring image spillovers in umbrella-branded products. *The Journal of Business, 63*(3), 309–329.

Thirumalai, S., & Sinha, K. K. (2011). Product recalls in the medical device industry: An empirical exploration of the sources and financial consequences. *Management Science, 57*(2), 376–392.

Trendel, O., Mazodier, M., & Vohs, K. D. (2018). Making warnings about misleading advertising and product recalls more effective: An implicit attitude perspective. *Journal of Marketing Research, 55*(2), 265–276.

Van Heerde, H., Helsen, K., & Dekimpe, M. G. (2007). The impact of a product-harm crisis on marketing effectiveness. *Marketing Science, 26*(2), 230–245.

Wang, X., & Wang, Z. (2014). The effect of product-harm crisis situations on firms' spokesperson strategies: Evidence from China's emerging market economy. *Public Relations Review, 40*, 110–112.

Wowak, K. D., Ball, G. P., Post, C., & Ketchen, D. J., Jr. (2021). The influence of female directors on product recall decisions. *Manufacturing & Service Operations Management, 23*(4), 895–913.

Wowak, K. D., Craighead, C. W., Ketchen, D. J., Jr., & Connelly, B. L. (2022). Food for thought: Recalls and outcomes. *Journal of Business Logistics, 43*, 9–35.

6

Industry Differences

> **What to Expect in This chapter**
> - This chapter delves into the particulars of product recall management across various industries, focusing on the consumer products sector, the food industry, and the vehicle industry.
> - It provides a comprehensive analysis of the common causes behind product recalls, available remedial measures, and effective communication strategies with both retailers and consumers within each industry.
> - Furthermore, it examines case studies and statistical data to underscore the far-reaching consequences of product recalls across diverse industrial landscapes.

The significance of recalls varies significantly across different industries. Not only do the causes of recalls differ substantially, but the regulatory framework within each product category also exhibits significant variation. This diversity is further reflected in the fact that different authorities often oversee regulation within each industry. Given the frequency of recalls, the volume of affected products, and the associated costs, including insurance expenses (refer Fig. 6.1), three industries stand out: consumer goods (i.e., IT, electronics, and domestic appliances), food, and automobiles. Recent research has predominantly concentrated on recalls within these three sectors (Astvansh et al., 2024). Consequently, we will delve extensively into these industries in the following three chapters.

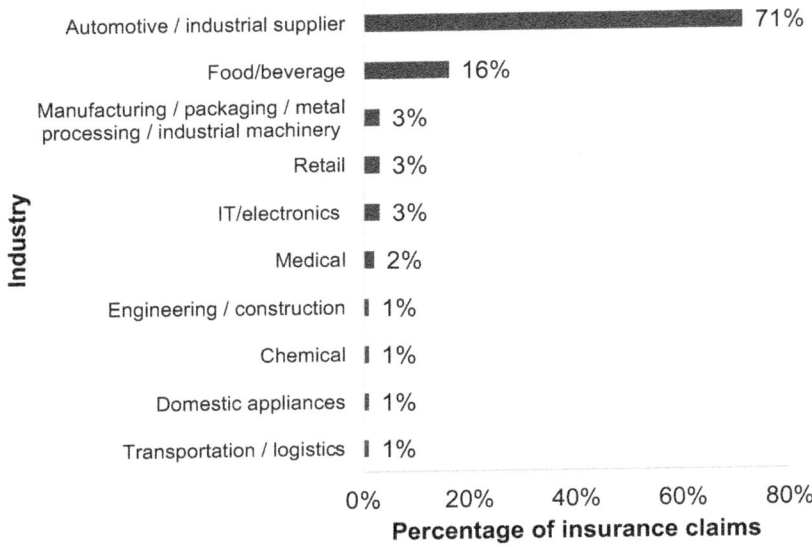

Fig. 6.1 Impacted industries by value of product recall insurance claims. Source: Own illustration based on data from Allianz (2017b)

6.1 Consumer Products

In most jurisdictions, consumer products cover a wide array of items, excluding those in sectors like automotive, aviation, pharmaceuticals, tobacco, food, and weaponry. This category boasts a vast assortment of products, ranging from household essentials like electronics, tools, and furniture to leisure items such as toys and sports gear. The consumer product industry is very diverse, presenting various complexities in materials, manufacturing processes, and product types.

Navigating recalls within this diverse landscape is no easy feat. Remedial actions can vary significantly, offering full solutions like free repairs, exchanges, refunds, or upgrades, or partial remedies such as repair kits or discounts. Contrast this with industries like automotive or food, where repairs (cars) or refunds (food) are the go-to responses. Selecting the appropriate remedy is a critical and intricate decision, with far-reaching implications for a company's performance, both financially and non-financially (e.g., Mafael et al., 2022; Raithel & Hock, 2021). For example, Fig. 3.6 in Sect. 3.2 illustrates that different remedial options, depending on severity and brand reputation, are more or less beneficial for retaining customer satisfaction.

Figuring out the best course of action becomes even more challenging due to the complex global supply chains inherent in the consumer product realm. These chains involve multiple players—suppliers, manufacturers, distributors, and retailers—making coordination and tracing defective products back to their source a daunting task Downstream traceability presents its own set of hurdles. Unlike perishable food items, consumer products endure for years, potentially posing risks to consumers long after purchase. Complicating matters further, many manufacturers distribute their products through third-party retailers, making direct communication with end-users difficult, if not impossible.

However, advancements in technology, particularly in Internet connected devices like smartphones and computers, offer some relief. Manufacturers can leverage these devices to communicate directly with users, as demonstrated by Samsung's approach, as detailed in Fig. 4.3 in Sect. 4.2.

Even for manufacturers selling directly through their own stores, challenges persist. Cash transactions or data privacy regulations may hinder direct communication with customers, leaving companies to navigate recall efforts through indirect channels.

The IKEA tip-over product recall, discussed in Sect. 3.1, illustrates these challenges vividly, showcasing how the company tackled issues of traceability and notification within the complex consumer product landscape.

IKEA's Tip-Over Issue (Revisited)

The IKEA tip-over issue primarily impacted dressers and chests, notably those from the longstanding MALM series, which have been globally available for decades. Safety concerns arose due to tip-over incidents, especially regarding the risk posed to children. Sadly, several deaths, dating back to 1989, were associated with tip-over accidents involving IKEA dressers and chests. While the likelihood of a fatal tip-over accident is relatively low, the extensive sales of these IKEA products, reaching tens of millions worldwide, underscore the gravity of the risk. This issue had a more significant impact in North America, where IKEA initiated an official product recall, while other countries, except China, did not follow suit due to differing regulatory and legal frameworks.

> Initially, IKEA launched a repair program, providing anchoring kits to secure furniture to walls, aiming to mitigate tip-over risks. Despite these efforts, incidents persisted, prompting IKEA to reassess its strategy. One challenge was that many consumers either failed to notice or disregarded IKEA's warnings. Additionally, reaching all customers with recalled products proved difficult.
>
> In response, IKEA introduced a *mandatory* product registration policy for certain items labeled as "Secure It!" products in North America (ikea-usa.com/safe). This initiative ensured consumers properly anchored furniture and served as a preventive measure against potential legal liabilities in the event of future tip-overs. Additionally, an optional registration for all durable IKEA products aimed to provide timely recall and safety information directly to consumers (info.ikea-usa.com/registration). IKEA also publishes all recalls on its website (ikea.com/us/en/customer-service/product-support/recalls/).
>
> In summary, the IKEA tip-over product recall spanned several years and involved millions of recalled units. Numerous incidents, including injuries and fatalities, led IKEA to provide anchoring kits initially and later implement mandatory and optional product registration systems to promote safety awareness, prevent future accidents, and enhance recall readiness.

The number of consumer product recalls remained relatively stable until 2023, when a significant increase was observed in both the EU and the USA, surpassing 4,000 recalls in both regions (refer to Fig. 6.2). In

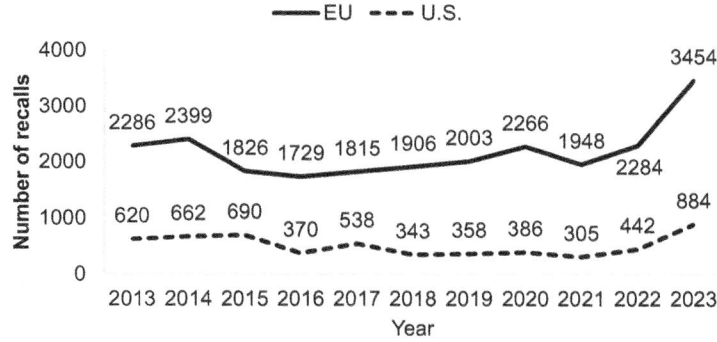

Fig. 6.2 Number of consumer product recalls in the EU and USA. Source: Own illustration based on data from the EU rapid alert system (ec.europa.eu/safety-gate-alert) and the USA. Consumer Product Safety Commission (cpsc.gov/recalls)

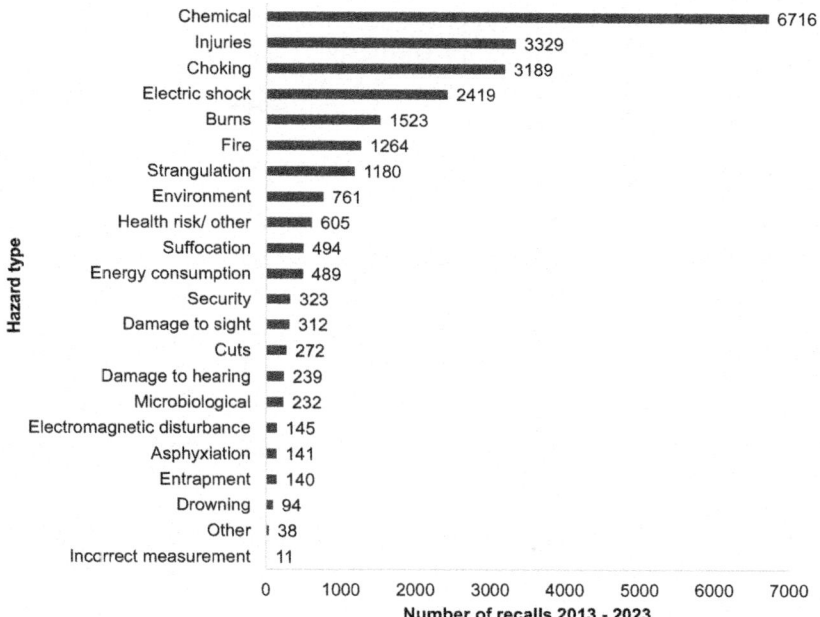

Fig. 6.3 Number of consumer product recalls in the EU by hazard type. Source: Own illustration based on data from the EU rapid alert system for dangerous non-food products (ec.europa.eu/safety-gate-alert)

2023, the USA witnessed 884 consumer product recalls, involving over 300 million product units. This equates to an average of approximately 2.4 recalled products per household in the USA, affecting all households, totaling about 127 million.

The reasons behind consumer product recalls are varied, but a few hazards stand out as the primary culprits for the majority of recalls. In the EU, these dominant reasons, accounting for 72% of recalls between 2013 and 2023, include contamination with chemicals (e.g., cancerous substances), injuries (e.g., furniture tip-overs), choking hazards (e.g., small parts breaking from toys), electric shocks (due to insufficient isolation of electrical appliances), and fire and burns (e.g., arising from overheating of electrical devices). Figure 6.3 provides an overview of all hazard types for consumer product recalls in the EU from 2013 to 2023.

One potential reason for the escalating number of consumer product recalls is the evolving regulatory landscape. Consumer product regulation, especially in the EU, is witnessing a surge, necessitating companies' careful attention in navigating and potentially adapting partner and vendor agreements to meet compliance standards and mitigate risks. The year 2023 marked a notable uptick in regulatory activity within the consumer products industry (Sedgwick, 2024).

A noteworthy development was the provisional agreement on the Ecodesign for Sustainable Products Regulation (ESPR) by the European Parliament and European Council, aligning with the EU's Circular Economy Action Plan under the European Green Deal. This regulation imposes extensive performance and information requirements on companies regarding their products' environmental footprint, covering aspects like reliability, repairability, energy efficiency, and recycled content. Particularly impactful is the ban on the destruction of textile products such as clothing and footwear, significantly affecting the textile industry.

Furthermore, consumer product companies face heightened legal risks due to the EU Representative Actions Directive, which harmonizes class action regimes across EU Member States. Additionally, the revised EU Product Liability Directive, pending approval, empowers consumers to seek compensation for damages caused by products, with added protections concerning software, artificial intelligence, and online marketplaces.

Online marketplaces are also subject to new regulations, including the EU General Product Safety Regulation, which strengthens liability and safety requirements for online sellers, necessitating product safety assessments, mandatory accident reporting, and product traceability.

Moreover, in the UK, proposed legislation called the Digital Markets, Competition, and Consumers Bill aims to enhance consumer protections online by granting authority to the Competition and Market Authority (CMA) and imposing specific obligations on large digital companies regarding trust, transparency, fair dealing, and open choice.

6.2 Food Industry

Unlike in the consumer products realm, where both full (such as free repair, exchange, and refund) and partial (like free repair kits) remedies are common, the standard practice in the food industry is to offer a full remedy (refund). However, part of the responsibility falls on customers, as they are typically required to return the products to the seller to obtain a refund (Raithel et al., 2023).

There are three primary reasons behind food recalls: manufacturing faults, design-related issues, and supply chain concerns. Manufacturing-related problems may stem from defects arising from pathogens or foreign materials. Common issues in this category include bacterial contamination with pathogens like listeria or salmonella, which can lead to food poisoning. According to reports, contamination emerged as the predominant factor behind food recalls in the UK and Europe during the first three quarters of 2023, accounting for nearly 2140 incidents out of approximately 4700 recalls in total (see Fig. 6.4). Other manufacturing-related reasons include the presence of foreign objects like plastic or metal in the product, unsanitary facilities and equipment, violation of import

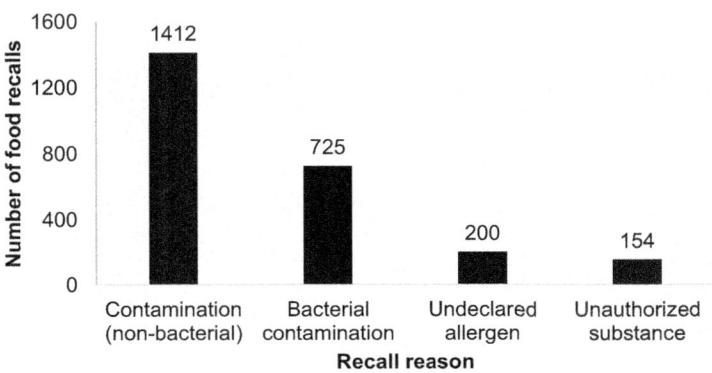

Fig. 6.4 Most frequent food recall reasons in the UK and Europe in the first three quarters of 2023. Source: Own illustration based on data from Sedgwick (2023)

and export rules, defects in processed food, and producing products requiring inspection coverage outside approved hours (FSA, 2023).

Design-related problems arise when safety standards are not met, particularly during packaging and labeling stages. Issues such as mislabeling or misbranding can compromise the authenticity of food products, potentially leading to consumer confusion or health risks. Incorrect or missing allergen information is another common design-related concern, especially in multi-ingredient products where various raw materials are sourced from different facilities and farms. Reports indicate that undeclared allergens were the primary reason for FDA recalls in the initial three quarters of 2023, accounting for 190 recalls out of a total of 401 (Sedgwick, 2023). The Stew Leonard recall of mislabeled cookies (see case study in Sect. 4.4) serves as a notable example highlighting the significance of mislabeling issues.

Product recalls linked to the supply chain often involve defects that arise from defect pre-products (e.g., use of banned pesticides by farmers) or occur during transportation, storage, and distribution processes. Issues during food transportation, such as failures in temperature control, can result in spoilage or contamination. Additionally, the increasing complexity of modern supply chains can impede the quick identification of affected products. For instance, the recall process for approximately 80% of the USA's food is slow, sometimes taking up to 10 months, even when people are falling ill (O'Donnell, 2017). Research suggests that dealing with numerous systems and suppliers can hinder producing firms. It is advised that companies refrain from frequent supplier changes based solely on cost considerations. Moreover, delays in response may occur due to lack of preparation or absence of recall plans. To avert such scenarios, managers should ensure suppliers meet standards (Wowak et al., 2022).

Figure 6.5 illustrates the top recalled product categories in the UK and Europe during the first three quarters of 2023. Fruits and vegetables were the most frequently recalled product category with 585 recalls. Nut products and seeds and dietetic foods, food supplements, and fortified foods followed as the second and third most-impacted categories, respectively. In terms of the highest number of recall notifications, Germany and the Netherlands led with 457 and 385 notifications, respectively.

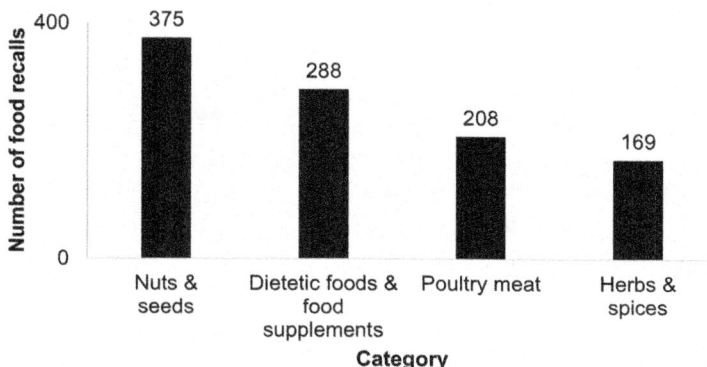

Fig. 6.5 Most recalled food categories in the UK and Europe in the first three quarters of 2023. Source: Own illustration based on data from Sedgwick (2023)

Communication with consumers in this sector is typically indirect. Regulatory agencies update recall notifications on their websites, retail stores issue recall notices, and mass media and social media platforms also play significant roles during recalls. Recall information can be shared via individual retailer shopper's club cards. Retailers with robust programs can notify their customers about recalled products they might have purchased. However, if consumers do not buy items from these retailers or if the recall fails to make national news, most recalls remain unknown to the general public. Although government websites and social media platforms publish such information, only proactive consumers who sign up for alerts will be informed through these channels. Moreover, given the vast number of grocery shoppers, the proportion of the population receiving these notices is likely to be quite low (Coffman & Baum, 2022).

Food that is on or likely to be on the market should be appropriately labeled or identified to enable traceability through relevant information. This is particularly crucial in this sector, where reaching customers individually proves challenging. However, the food industry faces several challenges for successful traceability implementation (Fisher, 2016; iTrade Insights, 2021), including:

- Lack of data: Insufficient record-keeping or absence of digitized data often leads to human errors and slow traceability.
- Limited visibility: Without shared or unified data, both buyers and suppliers struggle to achieve the necessary end-to-end visibility, crucial for identifying compromised goods quickly.
- Lack of coordination: Inefficient data and restricted visibility lead to deficiencies in coordination and collaboration. With intricate supply chains, coordination across the entire pathway becomes increasingly critical.
- Overlapping demands: Conflicting demands from national regulators worldwide complicate matters, along with diverse regulations regarding allergens, trace elements, pesticides, and other factors. Additionally, food fraud and market substitution pose global challenges.

In summary, businesses in the food and beverage industry face a shifting landscape marked by changing sustainability expectations and the need to address unethical practices. To ensure product authenticity, maintain customer confidence and health, and contribute to environmental protection, these companies should actively engage in sustainability discussions, prioritize robust traceability systems, and stay informed about regulatory developments.

6.3 Vehicle Industry

The use of vehicles poses significant health risks for both passengers and others on the road. According to the World Health Organization, over a million people die annually due to vehicle crashes, with millions more sustaining non-fatal injuries (WHO, 2023). Research suggests that vehicle recalls have the potential to substantially reduce the incidence of injuries and fatalities on the road (Bae & Benítez-Silva, 2011). Once potentially hazardous vehicles are repaired, they no longer pose a threat, thus eliminating a cause of incidents and accidents.

Recalls in the vehicle industry are frequent and widespread. Many manufacturers consistently face an ongoing series of recalls with varying levels of severity. In the USA, on of the largest vehicle market in the world, the yearly number of recalled vehicles reached approximately 31 million in 2022, representing a more than 50% increase over the last decade (NHTSA, 2023). Additionally, vehicle recalls incur substantial costs. Allianz, an insurance company, analyzed product recall insurance claims from January 2012 to June 2017, revealing that the automotive sector accounted for over 70% of the total value of losses examined, making it the costliest category in the analysis (Allianz, 2017b).

Moreover, the vehicle industry is associated with numerous high-profile recalls, resulting in significant adverse consequences for both affected customers and the manufacturers issuing the recalls. A notable example of such impactful recalls is the Takata airbag case:

> **Takata Corps Exploding Airbags**
>
> The timeline of the Takata airbag recalls underscores the potential magnitude of recalls in the vehicle industry for customers, suppliers, manufacturers, and other stakeholders. In November 2008, Honda recalled 4,000 vehicles due to the risk of explosion of the installed airbags manufactured and supplied by Takata Corp, a Japanese airbag manufacturer. Tragically, in May 2009, the first fatality caused by the defective airbags was reported when an 18-year-old woman died in her Honda Accord. Metal fragments ejected from the exploded Takata airbag severed her carotid artery (Klayman & Geoghegan, 2015).
>
> Since Honda's initial recall in 2008, multiple major recalls by the majority of vehicle manufacturers have ensued. In 2017, Takata Corp filed for bankruptcy due to liability costs associated with multiple fatalities and injuries (Hals, 2018). As of early 2024, the recall is ongoing, with approximately 67 million vehicles recalled by various manufacturers. In the USA, the NHTSA confirmed 27 deaths and over 400 injuries due to explosions of the defective airbags.
>
> Despite recall-specific communication efforts by the NHTSA (see Fig. 6.6), the press, and involved manufacturers, as of 2023, roughly 11 million defective airbags remain unreplaced, posing a threat to consumer health (e.g., Navarro & Beene, 2021; Ford, 2024; Honda, 2024; NHTSA, 2024). The NHTSA even launched a specific website to inform about the Takata airbag recalls and initiated advertising campaigns to raise awareness of the issue.
>
> The overall costs of the Takata airbag recalls have been estimated at $25 billion so far (Allianz, 2017a).

Fig. 6.6 Takata Airbag Recall advertising by the NHTSA. Source: Snapshot from YouTube video from Sedgwick (youtube.com/watch?v=y2yJ27ROjVg&t)

Recalls within the vehicle industry exhibit a wide variation in defect types and severity. Table 6.1 provides examples of defective vehicle components that could trigger a recall, ranging from malfunctioning back-up cameras to faulty airbags with potentially fatal consequences. Research indicates that the severity of hazards associated with recalled vehicles significantly influences the outcomes and management of recalls. Recalls due to high-severity defects elicit stronger negative stock price reactions compared to recalls involving milder defects (Bernon et al., 2018). Additionally, recalls with high hazard severity are generally more effective, with higher compliance rates, than those with low hazard severity (Rupp & Taylor, 2002; Malec et al., 2021). This suggests that customers are more likely to heed the manufacturer's recall instructions and get their vehicles repaired when faced with severe and potentially dangerous defects.

Unlike other sectors (e.g., consumer products), managers in the automotive industry must comply with numerous laws and regulations when handling recalls. In the USA, vehicle manufacturers are *mandated* to provide a full remedy to customers affected by recalls involving vehicles that are 15 years old or newer. This typically entails offering a free repair,

Table 6.1 Examples of potential reasons for vehicle recalls

Manufacturer	Year	NHTSA campaign	Defective component	Potentially affected vehicles	Exemplary recall description by manufacturer
Volkswagen	2018	18V148000	Airbags	363.713	*"Upon deployment of the driver's frontal airbag, excessive internal pressure may cause the inflator to explode"*
Tesla	2021	21V00D000	Back over prevention	356.309	*"The rearview camera cable harness may be damaged by the opening and closing of the trunk lid, preventing the rearview camera image from displaying"*
Kia	2020	20V750000	Engine	294.756	*"An engine compartment fire can occur while driving"*
Nissan	2021	21V957000	Fuel system	24.793	*"Abnormal wear inside the fuel pump may cause it to overheat and fail"*
Porsche	2018	18V841000	Brakes	112	*"The brake lines installed on the front axle may corrode over time. Corrosion inside the line may affect the front braking performance"*

Source: Own illustration based on data from U.S. NHTSA (nhtsa.gov/recalls)

replacing the affected vehicle, or reimbursing the full purchase price with a reasonable deduction for depreciation. Manufacturers generally opt for a free repair of the defect (NHTSA, 2017). In Germany, although a full remedy is not legally required, manufacturers typically choose to offer a free repair at local dealers to mitigate the reputational damage of the recall to the firm (Heimgärtner & Baumgarten, 2023).

Another regulation concerns the notification of customers affected by vehicle recalls. In the USA, vehicle recalls must be communicated by first-class mail, including a description of the hazard, the offered remedy, and instructions to schedule an appointment with the dealer (NHTSA, 2017). Fig. 4.2 in Sect. 4.4 shows an example of an owner notification letter. In Germany, this direct recall communication is conducted either by the vehicle manufacturer involved or by the Federal Motor Transport Authority (Kraftfahrt-Bundesamt, 2021). Similarly, in China, vehicle manufacturers are obligated to notify affected customers via registered letter and must communicate the recall through various media channels to the public (State Administration for Market Regulation, 2024).

Compared to other industries, vehicle recalls are generally more effective on average. In the U.S. vehicle industry, the average annual recall effectiveness, or recall compliance rate, has fluctuated between 52% and 73% over the last decade (NHTSA, 2023). In contrast, recall effectiveness in the consumer product category averages only 6% (CPSC, 2017). Direct communication with affected customers via first-class mail significantly contributes to the higher recall effectiveness in the vehicle industry. Vehicle owners typically register their vehicles upon purchase, allowing manufacturers to contact them directly by sending a letter. This direct communication increases recall effectiveness substantially compared to reliance solely on press releases (CPSC, 2017).

The higher effectiveness of vehicle recalls can also be attributed to other industry-specific factors. Firstly, vehicles are higher priced than products in other categories, motivating customers to comply with recalls as the potential benefits are greater. Additionally, recall effectiveness seems to depend on the value of the vehicle, with luxury vehicles and newer models exhibiting higher effectiveness (Malec et al., 2021).

Despite the higher recall effectiveness in the automotive industry, millions of recalled but unrepaired vehicles remain on the road, posing potential risks of future incidents and accidents. Implementing measures to further enhance recall effectiveness, such as simplifying appointment scheduling with local dealers and providing replacement vehicles during repairs, could mitigate these risks and reduce harm to both affected customers and recalling firms (Pagiavlas et al., 2022). Managers adopting such measures could effectively minimize the negative impact of recalls on both customers and firms (Bae & Benítez-Silva, 2011; Crosley, 2020; von Schlieben-Troschke & Raithel, 2023, 2024).

References

Allianz. (2017a, December 5). *Product recall risks growing in size and number as technology drives new triggers, warns Allianz.* Retrieved April 15, 2024, from https://www.allianz.com/en/press/news/business/insurance/171205-agcs-product-recall-risks-report.html.

Allianz. (2017b). *Product Recall: Managing the Impact of The New Risk Landscape.* Retrieved February 5, 2024, from https://commercial.allianz.com/content/dam/onemarketing/commercial/commercial/reports/AGCS-Product-Recall-Report.pdf.

Astvansh, V., Antia, K., & Tellis, G. (2024). Product recall: A synthesis of multidisciplinary findings, and research directions. *Marketing Letters.* https://doi.org/10.1007/s11002-024-09721-x

Bae, Y. K., & Benítez-Silva, H. (2011). Do vehicle recalls reduce the number of accidents? The case of the US car market. *Journal of Policy Analysis and Management, 30*(4), 821–862.

Bernon, M., Bastl, M., Zhang, W., & Johnson, M. (2018). Product recalls: The effects of industry, recall strategy and hazard, on shareholder wealth. *International Journal of Business Science & Applied Management (IJBSAM), 13*(1), 1–14.

Coffman, V. & Baum M. D. (2022). Modernizing recalls is a must for consumer safety. *Food Safety Magazine.* Retrieved March 17, 2024, from https://www.food-safety.com/articles/7780-modernizing-recalls-is-a-must-for-consumer-safety.

Consumer Product Safety Commission. (2017). *Recall effectiveness workshop (early session).* Retrieved April 16, 2024, from https://www.cpsc.gov/s3fs-public/Recall_Effectiveness_Workshop-Transcripts-2018. pdf?DANfPWVdXLz6jk.lAn9rzT3dX6ZQXQa0.

Crosley, T.(2020, March 19). Who's liable when a recalled product causes an injury?. Crosley Law. Retrieved April 15, 2024, from https://crosleylaw.com/blog/dangerous-defects-whos-liable-when-a-recalled-product-causes-an-injury/.

Fisher, W. (2016). Challenges of food traceability. *Food Safety Magazine*. Retrieved March 17, 2024, from https://www.food-safety.com/articles/4981-challenges-of-food-traceability.

Food Standards Agency. (2023, February 21). *Recalls and alerts*. Retrieved April 15, 2024, from https://www.food.gov.uk/about-us/recalls-and-alerts.

Ford. (2024). *Takata airbag recall*. Retrieved April 16, 2024, from https://www.ford.com/support/category/service-maintenance/frequently-asked-questions-regarding-takata-airbag-inflator-recalls/.

Hals, T. (2018, February 17). Judge approves Takata's U.S. bankruptcy plan. Reuters. Retrieved April 15, 2024, from https://www.reuters.com/article/idUSKCN1G10SW/.

Heimgärtner, K., & Baumgarten, A. (2023, November 8). Ihre Rechte bei Rückruf und Produkthaftung. *ADAC*. Retrieved April 16, 2024, from https://www.adac.de/rund-ums-fahrzeug/auto-kaufen-verkaufen/neuwagen-kauf/rechte-rueckrufaktion/#.

Honda. (2024, April 5). *Takata airbag inflator recall fact sheet*. Retrieved April 15, 2024, from https://hondanews.com/en-US/honda-corporate/releases/takata-airbag-inflator-recall-fact-sheet.

iTrade Insights. (2021). Closing food safety gaps: The 3 challenges of food traceability. Retrieved March 17, 2024, from https://www.itradenetwork.com/resources/closing-food-safety-gaps-the-3-challenges-of-food-traceability.

Klayman, B. & Geoghegan, I. (2015, May 20). *Timeline: Takata air bag recalls*. Reuters. Retrieved April 9, 2024, from https://www.reuters.com/article/us-autos-takata-takata-idUSKBN0O42QX20150520.

Kraftfahrt-Bundesamt. (2021, September 6). *Kodex zur Durchführung von Rückrufaktionen.* https://www.kba.de/DE/Themen/Marktueberwachung/Rueckrufe/Kodex/kodex_pdf.pdf. Accessed April 16, 2024.

Mafael, A., Raithel, S., & Hock, S. J. (2022). Managing customer satisfaction after a product recall: The joint role of remedy, brand equity, and severity. *Journal of the Academy of Marketing Science, 50*(1), 174–194.

Malec, A. M., Smith, P. K., & Smuts, A. E. (2021). Recall and vehicle characteristics associated with vehicle repair rates. *Review of Industrial Organization, 59*(1), 37–55.

National Highway Traffic Safety Administration. (2017). *Motor vehicle safety defects and recalls: What every vehicle owner should know.* https://www.nhtsa.gov/sites/nhtsa.gov/files/documents/mvdefectsandrecalls_808795.pdf. Accessed April 15, 2024.

National Highway Traffic Safety Administration. (2023). *NHTSA 2022 annual report safety recalls.* https://www.nhtsa.gov/sites/nhtsa.gov/files/2023-03/2022-Recalls-Annual-Report_030223-tag.pdf. Accessed April 15, 2024.

National Highway Traffic Safety Administration. (2024). *Takata recall spotlight.* https://www.nhtsa.gov/vehicle-safety/takata-recall-spotlight. Accessed April 15, 2024.

Navarro, A. & Beene, R. (2021, August 25). Takata's ticking time bomb is still on the road. Bloomberg. Retrieved May 15, 2024, from https://www.bloomberg.com/news/articles/2021-08-25/takata-air-bag-recall-millions-remain-defective-and-on-roads-worldwide#xj4y7vzkg.

O'Donnell, J. (2017, December 26). Inspector general report: FDA food recalls dangerously slow, procedures deeply flawed. USA Today. Retrieved February 8, 2024, from https://eu.usatoday.com/story/news/politics/2017/12/26/inspector-general-report-fda-food-recalls-dangerously-slow-procedures-deeply-flawed/975701001/.

Pagiavlas, S., Kalaignanam, K., Gill, M., & Bliese, P. D. (2022). Regulating product recall compliance in the digital age: Evidence from the "Safe Cars Save Lives" campaign. *Journal of Marketing, 86*(5), 135–152.

Raithel, S., & Hock, S. J. (2021). The crisis-response match: An empirical investigation. *Strategic Management Journal, 42*(1), 170–184.

Raithel, S., Hock, S. J., & Mafael, A. (2023). Product recall effectiveness and consumers' participation in corrective actions. *Journal of Academy of Marketing Science,* 1–20.

Rupp, N. G., & Taylor, C. R. (2002). Who initiates recalls and who cares? Evidence from the automobile industry. *The Journal of Industrial Economics, 50*(2), 123–149.

Sedgwick. (2023). *Recall index report.* Retrieved April 8, 2024, from https://www.sedgwick.com/brandprotection/.

Sedgwick. (2024). *Recall index report.* https://www.sedgwick.com/brandprotection/. Accessed April 15, 2024.

State Administration for Market Regulation. (2024). *Measures for the implementation of the regulations on the administration of recall of defective automobile products.* Retrieved April 16, 2024, from https://www.gov.cn/zhengce/2020-11/03/content_5723712.htm.

von Schlieben-Troschke, J., & Raithel, S. (2023). The opportunity in product recalls: The impact of recall compliance on brand satisfaction. Proceedings of the European Marketing Academy, 52nd.

von Schlieben-Troschke, J., & Raithel, S. (2024). The financial performance impact of product recall compliance. Proceedings of the European Marketing Academy, 53rd.

World Health Organization. (2023). Road traffic injuries. Retrieved April 15, 2024, from https://www.who.int/news-room/fact-sheets/detail/road-traffic injuries#:~:text=Approximately%201.19%20million%20people%20 die,adults%20aged%205%E2%80%9329%20years.

Wowak, K. D., Craighead, C. W., Ketchen, D. J., Jr., & Connelly, B. L. (2022). Food for thought: Recalls and outcomes. *Journal of Business Logistics, 43*, 9–35.

7

Spillover Effect

What to Expect in This Chapter
- This chapter elucidates the concept of the spillover effect and the underlying reasons behind its occurrence.
- It delineates how product recalls can transcend the boundaries of the recalled items, impacting other products within the same brand/company, competitors, and B2B customers.
- Practical examples are provided to underscore the implications for managers across different scenarios.
- Additionally, the chapter highlights insights into strategies that businesses can deploy to mitigate the adverse consequences of product recalls.

Product recalls can trigger extensive repercussions for products not directly implicated in the recall. Any recall has the potential to impact other products and brands marketed by the recalling firm. Moreover, it can also affect competitors. This phenomenon, termed the spillover effect, occurs when perceptions of a brand or product are influenced by information not directly tied to the brand or product itself (Ahluwalia et al., 2001). However, research suggests that spillover effects are more likely to occur when two brands or products share significant similarities in terms of product attributes, market size, and country of origin (Borah & Tellis, 2016). During product recalls, brands that may mutually influence and engage within a competitive landscape include non-recalled products within the same brand or company and competing brands in the same category (Mackalski & Belisle, 2015). This broader impact underscores the importance of considering implications beyond the brand directly involved in the recall. Subsequent sections will delve into how the spillover effect extends to similar products and brands.

7.1 Spillover on Same-Company Products

The spillover effect can exert an impact on unaffected products under the same or a different brand name sold by the recalling company. This occurs because the unaffected products of a brand cannot be entirely shielded from the negative publicity surrounding the affected products and become "guilty by association." The Land O'Lakes butter recall serves as an excellent case study for comprehending short-term spillovers stemming from a product recall.

> **Land O'Lakes Butter Stick Recall**
>
> In July 2003, Land O'Lakes, a prominent producer of butter, margarine, and dairy products in the USA, voluntarily recalled 3500 items of salted butter sticks due to potential metal fragment contamination. This recall, spanning 22 states, garnered extensive media coverage across national, local, and popular online platforms. Despite the adverse publicity, the recall was well-managed, with no reported injuries or fatalities. The company maintained effective communication channels with the FDA and retailers, and there was no evidence of shortages in other Land O'Lakes products. In this scenario, any spillover effect that occurred transpired under the *most optimal* circumstances amidst negative news coverage.
>
> Upon analyzing sales data for the 4 weeks preceding and the 6 weeks following the recall, Mackalski and Belisle (2015) revealed that the repercussions of the recall extended to both Land O'Lakes margarine and the broader Land O'Lakes brand portfolio. Essentially, the sales of the entire Land O'Lakes family of products experienced a decline of 17% within a month following the butter recall.

Further research suggests that during a product-harm crisis, consumers adjust their demand expectations based on information about similar products, leading to a lowering of expectations regarding the quality of unaffected products. Consequently, this results in dissatisfaction and a decline in demand (Che et al., 2023).

In addressing sales losses incurred by the recalled brand family, managers can leverage the following insights:

- Consumers typically associate products with specific brands rather than categories.
- The Land O'Lakes recall case, along with research findings, highlights the dual nature of the branded-house strategy. While such a strategy capitalizes on positive associations within the brand family, it also renders the brand susceptible to negative spillovers from product recalls (Ahluwalia et al., 2001).
- Alternatively, a house-of-brands strategy offers greater resilience, particularly during crises (Aaker, 2004).

7.2 Spillover on Competitors

Closely related competitors, sharing similarities or common associations with the brand of the recalling firm in the consumer's mind, are susceptible to spillover effects. Damage to the association with a recalling brand can lead to collateral damage for the brands linked by this association (Mackalski & Belisle, 2015). However, research indicates that the extent of the spillover effect can be influenced by various factors, including marketing activities (van Heerde et al., 2007), country of origin (Borah & Tellis, 2016), product reliability (Liu & Varki, 2021), and recall strategy (Fang et al., 2024). These factors will be further explored in the subsequent discussion.

Utilizing marketing mix tools can assist brands in the ecosystem in addressing product harm crises (Cleeren et al., 2013). A notable example is the Kraft peanut butter recall, as already discussed in Sects. 3.3 and 5.3.1.

> **Kraft Peanut Butter Recall in Australia (Revisited)**
>
> In 1996, Kraft Australia encountered a significant crisis when its peanut butter was linked to salmonella poisoning. The recall of all Kraft-made peanut butter led to the shutdown of 70% of Australia's peanut butter market. The severity of the crisis was underscored by numerous reported cases of salmonella poisoning and consumer complaints.
>
> Kraft faced backlash for its sluggish response and was subjected to legal action by a law firm. All Kraft peanut butter brand distributions came to a complete halt for over 4 months, spanning from June 30 to November 17, 1996. After the product-harm crisis, Kraft allocated up to AU$3 million for national advertising to reintroduce its peanut butter brands.
>
> During the 5-month crisis, Kraft's competitor brand, Sanitarium, significantly increased its weekly advertising expenditure, spending 36 times more than the pre-crisis period. Within the initial 4 weeks after the crisis, Kraft brand sales plummeted by 59% compared to the preceding 4 weeks, while Sanitarium's sales tripled. This surge in Sanitarium's sales was partly attributed to its aggressive advertising campaign (van Heerde et al., 2007).
>
> However, Sanitarium made a strategic misstep by deciding to raise prices. Analysis suggests that *reducing* prices would have been more strategically advantageous for long-term market share gains against Kraft brands (van Heerde et al., 2007). This decision potentially made consumers feel exploited by Sanitarium. Disappointed consumers quickly returned to Kraft after the recall, indicating the significance of pricing strategies in maintaining consumer loyalty also throughout and after a competitor's product-harm crises.

An important insight from the Kraft case is that not only do negative spillovers extend to competitors, but a competitor can benefit from a (poorly managed) product recall (van Heerde et al., 2007). Research underscores that competitors have the potential to boost their short-term sales through advertising, coupons, promotions, and other tools during the crisis (Mackalski & Belisle, 2015).

As the product-harm crisis can damage whole product categories, category advertising and prices need to be adjusted depending on the nature of the product-harm crisis, the recalling firm's blame, and the negative publicity the crisis receives (Cleeren et al., 2013). Figure 7.1 summarizes general guidelines.

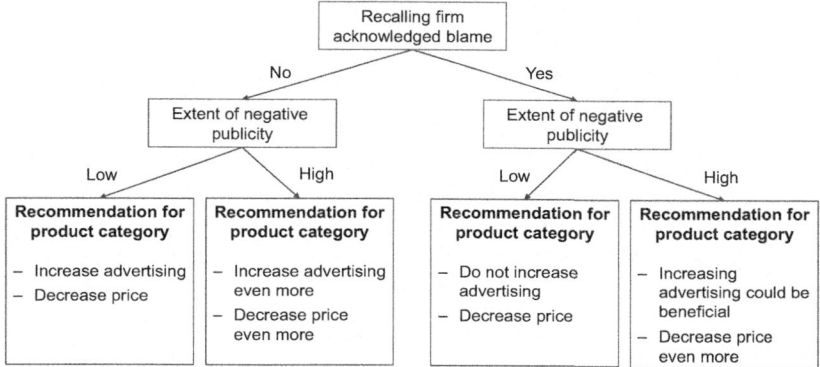

Fig. 7.1 Recommended post-recall measures for the category based on recall characteristics. Source: Own Illustration based on Cleeren et al. (2013)

Another key factor that can influence consumer perceptions of similarity between brands is the country of origin. Consumers may make similar assumptions about brands from the same country. For instance, consumers might believe that brands from the same country share similar product development processes. In fact, in many instances, brands from the same country use the same sourcing and production processes for product development (Borah & Tellis, 2016). One primary example in this regard is the Volkswagen emissions scandal, which is also described in Sects. 3.1 and 3.2.

> **Volkswagen's Dieselgate (Revisited)**
>
> In September 2015, Volkswagen admitted to installing a "defeat device" in certain diesel cars, which deactivated emission controls during regular driving but re-engaged them during tests. This allowed the vehicles to emit up to 40 times more pollution than allowed.
>
> In the initial 5 days of the recall, European competitors and suppliers connected to Volkswagen incurred 18.3 and 12.6 billion euros in abnormal losses, respectively. European competitors such as Daimler, BMW, and Renault experienced the most substantial individual abnormal losses in the market values (Barth et al., 2022). Other research findings indicate that negative online chatter is strongest among brands from the same country and influences performance metrics, like sales and stock market performance, of rivals (Borah & Tellis, 2016).

Accordingly, close monitoring of recall incidents involving competitors from the same country and with a similar target segment is warranted. Further, competitors should analyze how their own brands relate to the rival and the rival's recall. Based on this analysis, the competitor must align its strategy, which lets the competitor either benefit from the recall (see Kraft example above) or go for actions that minimize the negative spillover to avoid becoming "guilty by association" and also suffering from the product-harm crisis (see Volkswagen Dieselgate). When minimizing the negative spillover effect, competitors should be cautious of adopting a denial strategy, asserting that a firm's sourcing, manufacturing, designs, and scientific procedures have no link to the focal recall (e.g., "We are clean."), which may eventually backfire.

Another crucial factor that amplifies the spillover effect of product recalls to competitors is the reputation of a firm for providing reliable products. For example, when Toyota recalled its vehicles in 2010, it led to market value losses of 1.63%, 1.96%, and 5.90% for Honda, Nissan, and Ford, respectively (Borah & Tellis, 2016). In 2014, when General Motors issued a recall, Honda, Ford, and Toyota only experienced losses of 0.19%, 0.87%, and 0.29%. Despite both companies recalling products, Toyota's recall had a more significant impact, possibly due to its perceived higher product reliability compared to General Motors.

Indeed, research indicates that product recalls result in a negative spillover effect on competitors' market value, particularly when the product reliability of the recalling firm is high. Nevertheless, this impact diminishes as the product reliability of the competitor increases (Liu & Varki, 2021). In this context, managers are advised to actively promote their product quality. For instance, if Toyota declares a product recall, Hyundai could counteract the fallout by highlighting that its Kia's Sorento and Rio models earned the 2018 Quality Award from J.D. Power.

The recalling firm's recalling strategy is the fourth important factor impacting the spillover effect of product recalls on competitors. A recalling firm may opt for one of the two primary strategies: proactive recall or passive recall. Proactive recall is initiated before any incidents involving harm for customers have happened. On the other hand, passive recalls are prompted after the firm receives information about incidents linked to defect product which usually goes along with pressure from the regulator to recall the product. In the eyes of customers, a firm is seen as more socially responsible, trustworthy, and customer-oriented when it takes proactive measures, before government agency intervention becomes necessary.

However, research demonstrates that proactive recalls result in more negative abnormal returns for competitors compared to passive recalls. Unlike customers, investors may perceive proactive recalls as an indication of significant product safety issues and potential financial losses for the recalling firm (Chen et al., 2009). Consequently, this can not only lead to a significant negative impact on the recalling firm's stock performance in the short term, but it can heighten investors' perceptions of risk across the entire industry, resulting in adverse effects spilling over to other competitors within the same sector (Fang et al., 2024). As a response, competitors can launch short-term advertising and promotional tactics to mitigate this negative impact. Such marketing investments can reinforce the trust of customers and investors in the competitor's product safety—the prerequisite is, however, that the competitor is not involved in similar product safety issues which backfire when becoming public.

Table 7.1 summarizes how the spillover effect extends to competitors. The table outlines key factors influencing the spillover effects of product recalls on competitors, providing insights into their impact and recommended strategies.

7.3 Spillover on B2B Customers

When a product is recalled due to safety concerns, quality issues, or regulatory violations, it not only affects end consumers but also ripples through the supply chain, impacting the recalling firm's B2B customers. These customers may rely on the recalled product as a component or ingredient in their own manufacturing processes, leading to changes in their operations. Singh (2021) found both negative spillover effects of recalls on other non-recalled items under the same brand in B2B markets within the vehicle industry. Specifically, non-recalled models within the same vehicle segment as the recalled model encounter decreased demand at B2B auctions, leading to approximately 5.54% lower prices.

Table 7.1 Summary of factors influencing spillover effects on competitors

Factors	Description	Impact on rivals	Recommendation for rivals
Marketing activities	Effective use of marketing mix tools by rivals during a poorly managed crisis by the recalling firm	– Benefit from increase in short-term sales	– Leverage promotional tools and advertising strategies
Country of origin	Consumer perceptions based on the origin of brands	– Suffer from decrease in sales and abnormal returns – Negative online chatter	– Manage online presence and communication during a competitor's recall – Avoid adopting a denial strategy
Product reliability	Reputation for providing reliable products	– High product reliability of the recalling firm: Negative effect on competitors' market value – High product reliability of the rival: Acts as a buffer and reduces the negative spillover impact	– Build and promote a strong reputation for product reliability
Recall strategy	Recalling firms' strategy (proactive vs passive)	– Proactive recalls cause more negative abnormal returns than passive recalls	– Initiate short-term advertising and promotional campaigns

Source: Own illustration

Non-recalled models from competing automakers, belonging to the same segment as the recalled model, also face reduced prices (approximately 5.63%) due to the spillover effect.

The reputational harm incurred by the recalling company can diminish the trust and confidence of its B2B partners. A prominent example is the impact of Boeing's quality problems on its B2B customers (see also case description in Sect. 3.1).

> **Boeing's Enduring Quality Issues (Revisited): Airlines' Reputational Damage**
>
> Boeing's manufacturing problems have become also a crisis for Alaska Airlines, along with its primary customer, United Airlines, as they rush to inspect their aircraft fleets and reassure worried passengers and shareholders.
>
> In an effort to rebuild its reputation and foster trust, Alaska Airlines implemented a rather assertive public relations strategy by inviting a camera crew into their hangar to conduct inspections on the aircraft and highlight the manufacturing flaws attributed to Boeing. It is worth noting that both airlines are placing a high priority on communicating with their customers. After the incident on January 5th 2024, Alaska Airlines CEO released a video message addressed to frequent flyers, detailing the events of Flight 1282, and apologizing for the tension caused. Further, he outlined the steps the airline will take to address any resulting flight disruptions, as Alaska has grounded approximately 20% of its fleet.
>
> United Airlines has also maintained consistent communication, expressing apologies to travelers for the cancellations and pledging that the 737 Max 9 aircraft "won't fly until they are approved and we are confident they are 100% safe" (Hawkins, 2024).

References

Aaker, D. A. (2004). *Brand portfolio strategy: Creating relevance, differentiation, energy, leverage, and clarity*. Simon & Schuster.

Ahluwalia, R., Unnava, H. R., & Burnkrant, R. E. (2001). The moderating role of commitment on the spillover effect of marketing communications. *Journal of Marketing Research, 38*(4), 458–470.

Barth, F., Eckert, C., Gatzert, N., & Scholz, H. (2022). Spillover effects from the Volkswagen emissions scandal: An analysis of stock and corporate bond markets. *Schmalenbach Journal of Business Research, 74*, 37–76.

Borah, A., & Tellis, G. J. (2016). Halo (spillover) effects in social media: Do product recalls of one brand hurt or help rival brands? *Journal of Marketing Research, 53*(2), 143–160.

Che, X., Katayama, H., & Lee, P. (2023). Product-harm crises and spillover effects: A case study of the Volkswagen diesel emissions scandal in eBay used car auction markets. *Journal of Marketing Research, 60*(2), 409–424.

Chen, Y., Ganesan, S., & Liu, Y. (2009). Does a firm's product-recall strategy affect its financial value?. An examination of strategic alternatives during product-harm crises. *Journal of Marketing, 73*(6), 214–226.

Cleeren, K., van Heerde, H. J., & Dekimpe, M. G. (2013). Rising from the ashes: How brands and categories can overcome product-harm crises. *Journal of Marketing, 77*(2), 58–77.

Fang, X., Wang, W., Shao, Y., & Banerjee, P. (2024). Examining the effect of a firm's product recall on financial values of its competitors. *Journal of Business Research, 176*. https://doi.org/10.1016/j.jbusres.2024.114586

Hawkins, E. (2024, January 25). Airlines blame Boeing for reputational damage. *Axios*. Retrieved April 15, 2024, from https://www.axios.com/2024/01/25/airlines-turn-on-boeing.

Liu, D., & Varki, S. (2021). The spillover effect of product recalls on competitors' market value: The role of corporate product reliability. *Journal of Business Research, 137*, 452–463.

Mackalski, R., & Belisle, J. F. (2015). Measuring the short-term spillover impact of a product recall on a brand ecosystem. *Journal of Brand Management, 22*, 323–339.

Singh, K. (2021). Essays on product recall decision and effect. https://doi.org/10.17615/s480-5j74.

Van Heerde, H., Helsen, K., & Dekimpe, M. G. (2007). The impact of a product-harm crisis on marketing effectiveness. *Marketing Science, 26*(2), 230–245.

8

Conclusion: Top 10 Key Takeaways and Outlook on Future Challenges

> **What to Expect in This Chapter**
>
> This chapter summarizes the Top 10 key takeaways of this book:
>
> 1. Product-harm crises and product recalls stand as unavoidable business risks.
> 2. It is imperative to address any potential (latent) product-harm crises proactively.
> 3. Consider both the immediate and enduring legal, non-financial, and financial ramifications.
> 4. A customer-centric approach defines successful product recall management.
> 5. Integrate product recall events and remediation seamlessly into the customer journey map.
> 6. Leverage product recalls as opportunities to showcase the firm's integrity and fortify trust.
> 7. Recall readiness serves as the linchpin for successful recall management.
> 8. Product recall management emerges as a pivotal element within the marketing strategy.
> 9. Adapting the recall management cycle to the business model and industry is important.
> 10. Continuously refine recall protocols to ensure effectiveness in a dynamic environment.
>
> This chapter concludes with an outlook on future challenges and developments relevant to product recall management.

In the vast realm of product management, the looming specter of non-compliance, safety issues, and recalls presents itself as an unavoidable business risk. However, merely acknowledging this risk and adopting a passive stance is far from a winning strategy. This book argues that firms not only should but also could manage this business risk proactively. Amidst the multifaceted considerations, several notable aspects warrant special attention.

While not every product hiccup escalates into a full-scale product-harm crisis or necessitates a comprehensive product recall management approach, each potential safety concern demands delicate handling—especially in an era of constant scrutiny and instantaneous global news dissemination. Even before any public outcry, every product failure and safety concern should be regarded as a latent product-harm crisis waiting to unfurl. In this dynamic landscape, managers must stay ahead of the curve, adeptly surfing the wave of information; hence, proactive behavior emerges as the preferred strategy over reactive measures.

Effective decision-making in this milieu necessitates a holistic assessment of both short- and long-term implications, encompassing legal, non-financial, and financial dimensions. Managers must prioritize maintaining a consistent cash flow, recognizing that any significant product-harm crisis can entail substantial financial burdens, including immediate recall costs and legal ramifications. While this short-term perspective is crucial for ensuring the firm's survival during a product-harm crisis, managers must also weigh potential long-term effects. Erosion of customer trust, damage to reputation, and tarnished brand images can impede long-term recovery efforts. For instance, BMW recently severed ties with its long-term supplier, Continental, following a significant recall affecting approximately 370,000 cars worldwide. This recall, stemming from faulty brakes supplied by Continental, incurred costs amounting to approximately 400 million EUR for BMW (Wallstreet Online, 2024).

Strategic research and practice offer a roadmap for navigating these turbulent waters. While acknowledging the diverse stakeholders involved—with customers and wholesalers/retailers holding primary stakes—a customer-centric approach to managing product-harm crises and recalls proves more effective than relying solely on legal or technical

8 Conclusion: Top10 Key Takeaways and Outlook on Future...

frameworks. This perspective extends beyond mere customer-centric strategies; it encompasses customer-centric product recall management.

Embedding product safety concerns and recall protocols into the fabric of business operations requires integrating them seamlessly into the customer journey and touchpoint management strategies. Achieving this integration mandates a deep understanding and implementation of the product management cycle. Figure 8.1 depicts a classic customer journey map augmented by the product recall event as another customer touchpoint.

Viewing the product recall event as another—equally important—customer touchpoint is perhaps the most important takeaway from this book, suggesting two key implications. First, successful customer relationship management throughout the customer journey necessitates a professional approach to product recall management—although the marketing process may need to be managed in reverse. Second, product harm-crisis and recalls are not inherently negative; they represent an opportunity to showcase the firm's true qualities and characteristics, echoing the words of the nineteenth-century born American novelist James Jane Allen: "Adversity does not build character—it reveals it."

At the heart of this endeavor lies the establishment of recall readiness. Waiting until a product-harm crisis strikes and a recall becomes imperative leaves scant room for meticulous planning or strategic deliberation. Thus, proactive measures to establish recall preparedness are indispensable. In this context, product recall management should become a cornerstone of any marketing strategy. While many successful firms boast elaborate customer satisfaction and relationship frameworks, the product recall event often remains inadequately addressed within these frameworks.

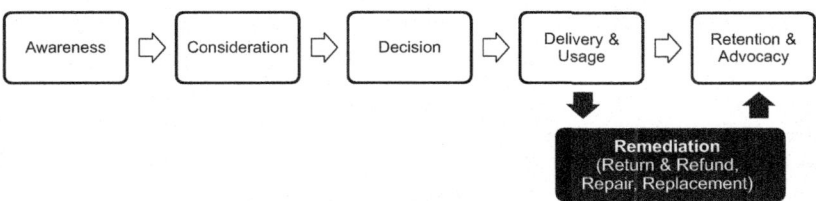

Fig. 8.1 Extending the customer journey map by the product recall event and remediation phase. Source: Own Illustration

The product recall management cycle (see Chap. 5 and Fig. 8.2) offers a comprehensive framework encompassing all relevant aspects and tasks.

However, adhering solely to a predefined cycle proves insufficient. Managers must possess the tools and insights to navigate each phase effectively. Every industry, business model, and supply chain presents unique intricacies requiring adaptation of the general product management cycle outlined herein. Nonetheless, the proposed cycle serves as a solid foundation, covering all pertinent aspects managers must consider when customizing it to their specific needs and strategies. In an ever-changing and dynamic market environment, it is crucial to continually refine recall protocols and adapt the recall management cycle to ensure effectiveness.

Product recall management is increasingly vital as it confronts a host of challenges in the coming years, driven by globalization, technological advancements, shifting consumer behaviors, and evolving regulatory environments and environmental concerns.

The globalization of supply chains presents a significant hurdle, with products now originating from diverse countries, complicating the tracking and retrieval of faulty items. Coordinating recalls across international borders brings about logistical and regulatory complexities. Moreover, modern supply chains are growing more intricate, featuring multiple tiers of suppliers and subcontractors. Pinpointing the precise source of a product defect and tracing it through this labyrinthine supply chain poses considerable challenges, particularly when dealing with sub-tier suppliers. To mitigate these risks, building resilience in supply chains becomes imperative. This entails strategies such as diversifying supplier networks, instituting robust quality control measures, and investing in real-time monitoring technologies.

The rise of the Internet of Things (IoT) introduces a new dimension to product safety. While digitalization offers early defect detection opportunities, it also introduces cybersecurity risks and data security concerns. Effectively managing the vast volumes of data generated by IoT devices necessitates robust data management and analytics capabilities. Organizations must invest in technologies and expertise to collect, analyze, and interpret data efficiently, aiding in the early identification of product defects and streamlining recall procedures.

8 Conclusion: Top10 Key Takeaways and Outlook on Future...

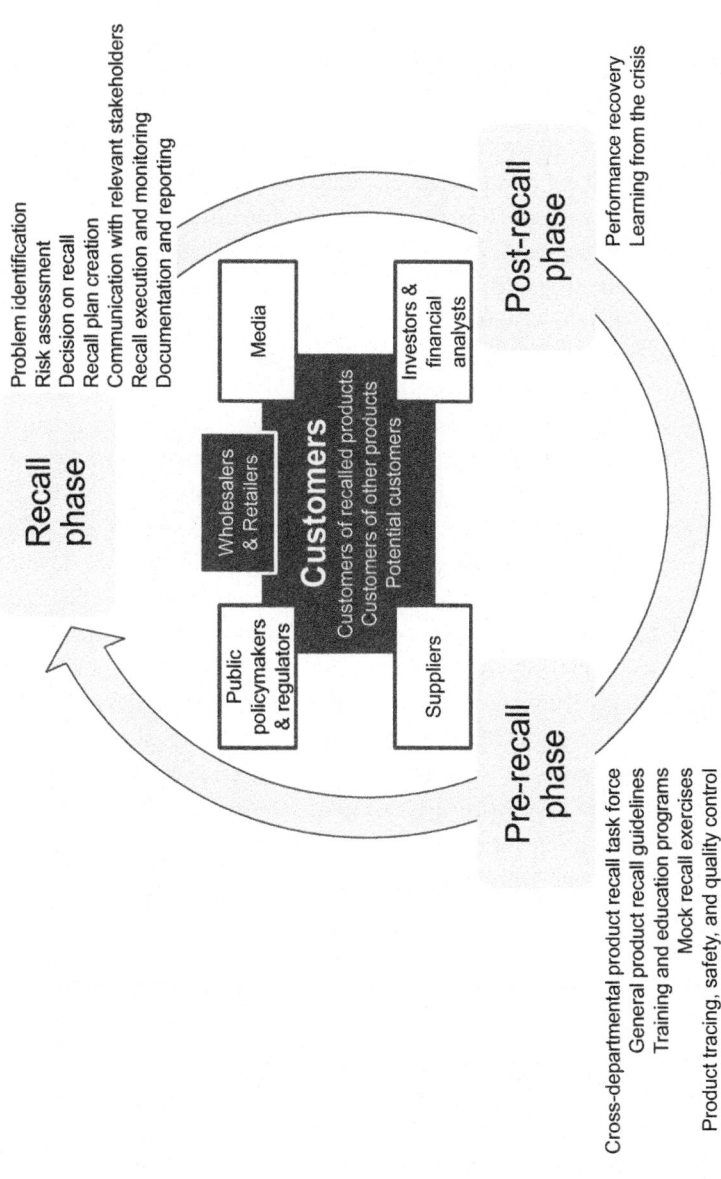

Fig. 8.2 The product recall management cycle. Source: Own illustration

Empowered customers, aided by Artificial (General) Intelligence (A(G)I) technologies, wield unprecedented influence. These technologies empower consumers not only to compare products but also to identify potential hazards swiftly. While A(G)I holds promise for preempting safety risks, it also accelerates the dissemination of safety-related information, impacting public perception via social media platforms. Managing public perception in real-time becomes paramount to mitigate reputational damage during recall events. A(G)I technologies offer many transformative opportunities for manufacturers, enhancing product safety across research, development, and production phases, while also facilitating improved safety issue identification, product tracing, and targeted customer engagement during recalls.

A(G)I presents also a significant legal and regulatory conundrum for manufacturers integrating this technology into their products. Questions arise regarding accountability in the event of, for instance, an accident involving an A(G)I-driven car: will responsibility lie with the human owner of the vehicle, or will it extend to the manufacturer who developed the A(G)I systems? This complex issue underscores the need for a comprehensive legal framework that addresses liability in the age of A(G)I. Current laws may not adequately account for the unique challenges posed by A(G)I-products, leaving ambiguities regarding accountability.

Navigating the regulatory landscape poses another significant challenge, with requirements varying across jurisdictions and industries. Multinational corporations must navigate these complexities through close collaboration with regulatory bodies, industry partners, and stakeholders. As regulatory frameworks evolve, placing greater emphasis on product compliance and safety, investments in recall management remain crucial.

While public attention currently focuses on safety risks and swift response to remove unsafe products from markets, the environmental implications of product recalls cannot be overlooked. Disposal or recycling of large quantities of recalled products can have significant environmental consequences. Organizations must consider the environmental impact of recalls and adopt sustainable disposal and recycling practices where feasible. It is inevitable that the public and NGOs will increasingly scrutinize the environmental impact of recalled products, eventually necessitating regulatory intervention.

In conclusion, managers entrusted with product safety and recall management must adopt a proactive approach, integrating these concerns into all aspects of their operations. Prioritizing customer-centric strategies, leveraging advanced technologies, and staying abreast of regulatory changes will enable organizations to navigate these challenges effectively, safeguarding brand reputation and customer trust.

Reference

Wallstreet Online. (2024, March 21). *BMW stellt Conti wegen Problemen bei Bremse vorerst aufs Abstellgleis.* https://www.wallstreet-online.de/nachricht/17911584-mm-bmw-stellt-conti-problemen-bremse-vorerst-aufs-abstellgleis. Accessed April 15, 2024.

Index

A

Accepting blame, 106
Accountability in the supply chain, 57
Activities during recall phase, 88–89
Advertising after a recall, 35, 36
Advertising during a recall, 35
Advertising effectiveness in the post-recall phase, 106
Advertising in the post-recall phase, 106
Agenda-setting Theory, 60
Alpha testing, 90
Ambivalence effect, 30
Approval by regulators, 54
Artificial General Intelligence, 150
Assessment of financial implications by investors and analysts, 63
Assessment of operational performance by investors and analysts, 63
Assessment of reputation management by investors and analysts, 63
Assistance of wholesalers and retailers, 50
Audi's poor root cause analysis 1986, 90
Automotive products, 126–131
   communication with customers, 130
   recall effectiveness, 130
   recall reasons, 128
   remedy, 128
Awareness for recall, 45

Index

B

Batch analysis, 58
Beta testing, 89
Boeing quality issues, 23, 87, 143
Boomerang effect, 30
Brand damage after product recall, 51
Brand hate, 29
Branding strategy, 137
Buffering effect, 30
Business performance, 146
Business risk, 146

C

Campbells traceability program, 85
Case study
   Audi's poor root cause analysis 1986, 90
   Boeing quality issues, 23, 87, 143
   Campbell's traceability program, 85
   crisis preparedness in airline industry, 76–78
   customized approach to global recall management, 73–75
   faulty gas grill kits, 27–28
   Fisher Price Rock 'n Play sleeper 2019 recall, 93–94
   Ford Pinto 1978 recall, 17–18
   GM faulty ignition switch 2014 recall, 46, 110
   IKEA tip over issue, 24, 119–120
   Intel 1994 Pentium processor defect, 70–71
   Johnson & Johnson 2010 phantom recall, 64
   Kinder chocolate 2022 and 2023 recalls, 4
   Kraft peanut butter 1996 recall, 36, 108, 138
   Kryptonite Bic pen crisis 2004, 61
   Land O'Lakes butter stick 2003 recall, 136
   Mattel toy 2007 recall, 5–6
   Mislabeled Vanilla Florentine cookies 2024, 59
   Peloton treadmill 2023 recall, 54
   Pepsi's fake product-harm crisis 1993, 92
   Samsung Galaxy Note 7 2016 recall, 51
   Space Shuttle Challenger 1986 disaster, 57
   Takata Corp airbag 2013 recall, 127
   Volkswagen's Dieselgate, 24–25, 31, 139
Characteristics of product recalls, 11
Chinese 2008 milk crisis, 1
Chipotle 2015 recall, 98
Civil liability, 22
Collaboration with regulators, 55
Common mistake in media relations, 62
Communication strategy, 96
Communication with customers
   automotive products, 130
   consumer products, 119
   customer hotline, 98
   food products, 125
   media, 103
   recall advertisiement, 100
   regulators, 102

retailers, 102
social media strategy, 98
spokesperson, 100
Communication with regulators during recall, 102
Communication with relevant stakeholders, 97–103
    low risk recall, 98
    precautionary recall, 98
    relevant information, 97
    secondary impact recall, 98
    voluntary recall, 98
Communication with retailers during recall, 102
Competitor response, 36
Complex regulatory landscape, 56
Components of recall readiness, 78
Conforming behavior, 32
Consumer products, 118–122
    communication with customers, 119
    food traceability, 125
    information requirement, 122
    legal risks, 122
    performance requirement, 122
    product registration, 120
    product traceability, 119
    recall reasons, 121
    regulatory landscape, 122
    remedy, 118
    supply chain, 119
Consumer Product Safety Act, 54
Continued sell of recalled items, 52
Contractual liability, 22
Contractual obligations of suppliers, 56
Coordination with wholesalers and retailers, 50

Costs of recalls
    direct, 19
    indirect, 19
Country of origin, 137, 139
Criminal liability, 22
Crisis management in airline industry, 76
Crisis preparedness in airline industry, 76–78
Cross-departmental product recall task force, 78–81
    customer-centric, 81
    diversity, 79
    external expertise, 79
    female managers, 79
    internal expertise, 79
    marketing expertise, 80
Customer-centric approach, 146
Customer-centric perspective, 70
Customer-centric product recall task force, 81
Customer disappointment, 29
Customer expectations behavior, 32
Customer hotline, 98
Customer journey management, 147
Customer-level recall, 14
Customers, 44–49
    awareness for recall, 45
    feedback, 44
    identification of recalled products, 45
    instructions, 44
    owner notification letter, 46
    recall alert, 44, 45
    recall notification, 44
    recommended action, 44
    safety message, 51
Customer satisfaction, 29

Customer satisfaction after a recall
   ambivalence effect, 30
   boomerang effect, 30
   buffering effect, 30
   opportunity effect, 30
   wipe-out effect, 30
Customer touchpoint management, 147
Customer trust, 146
Customized approach to global recall management, 73–75

D

Decision on recall, 91–94
Delta testing, 90
Denial strategy, 140
Direct costs, 34
Direct costs of recalls, 19
Distribution-level recall, 15
Distributors, 50–53
   assistance, 50
   coordination, 50
   early detection of product issues, 50
   product tracking, 50
   training and support, 50
Diversity of product recall task force, 79
Documentation and reporting, 104–105
Dual edged impact of media, 60

E

Early detection of product issues, 50
Edeka and Kaufland olive oil 2024 recall, 13
Emotional aspect of customer concerns, 71
Empowered customers, 150
Enforcing legal compliance, 54
Engagement with resale platforms, 53
Enhanced compliance program, 54
Environmental implications of recalls, 150
Escalating efforts by regulators, 54
Ethical considerations, 18, 19
External information sources, 89

F

Faulty gas grill kits, 27–28
Feedback, 44
Female managers in product recall task force, 79
Financial analysts, 63–65
   assessment of financial implications, 63
   assessment of operational performance, 63
   assessment of reputation management, 63
   long-term sustainability in light of the recall, 63
   proactive management, 64
   regulatory compliance, 63
   transparency, 64
Financial performance implications of recalls, 19, 34–37, 91
   direct costs, 34
   legal expenses, 34
   recall environment, 34
   reputation and trust damage, 34
   sales, 35

Firestorm, 61
Fisher Price Rock 'n Play sleeper 2019 recall, 53, 93–94
Food products, 123–126
    communication with customers, 125
    design related problems, 124
    manufacturing related problems, 123
    product categories, 124
    recall reasons, 123
    remedy, 123
    supply chain related problems, 124
Ford Pinto 1978 recall, 17–18
Full remedy, 29
Future challenges, 145–151
    artificial general intelligence, 150
    empowered customers, 150
    environmental implications of recalls, 150
    globalization, 148
    internet of things, 148
    regulatory landscape, 150
    technological advancements, 148

G

Gamma testing, 89
General product recall guidelines, 78, 81–82
    how-to handbook, 81
    ISO standard, 82
    product safety certification, 82
    regulatory guidelines, 82
    standardized procedures, 81
Globalization, 148
GM faulty ignition switch 2014 recall, 46, 110

Golden 24 hours rule, 61
Guilty by association-effect, 136, 140

H

Herding effects, 34
Hotline for direct customer feedback, 36
How-to handbook, 77, 81, 96

I

Identification of recalled products, 45
IKEA tip over issue, 24, 119–120
Implementing remedies, 103
Indirect costs of recalls, 19
Industry differences, 117–131
    automotive products, 126–131
    consumer products, 118–122
    food products, 123–126
Industry regulations, 94
Ineffective communication with retailers, 51
Influencers, 60
Innovation in the post-recall phase, 111
Instructions, 44
Intel 1994 Pentium processor defect, 70–71
Internal information sources, 89
Internet of Things, 148
Investors, 63–65
    assessment of financial implications, 63
    assessment of operational performance, 63
    assessment of reputation management, 63

Investors (*cont.*)
  long-term sustainability in light of the recall, 63
  negative overraction, 35
  proactive management, 64
  regulatory compliance, 63
  risk aversion, 35
  transparency, 64
Involuntary product recall, 12
Isolating returned items, 103

J

Johnson & Johnson 1982 Tylenol crisis, 64
Johnson & Johnson 2010 phantom recall, 64
Journalists, 60–63
  common mistake, 62
  intermediaries, 60
  stonewalling backfire, 62
  trustful relationship, 63

K

Key strategies in the post-recall phase, 106
Key takeaways, 145–151
Kinder chocolate 2022 and 2023 recalls, 4
Kraft peanut butter 1996 recall, 36, 108, 138
Kryptonite Bic pen crisis 2004, 61

L

Land O'Lakes butter stick 2003 recall, 136
Latent product-harm crisis, 14

Learning in the post-recall phase, 108–112
Legal expenses, 34
Legal liability implications of recalls, 21
Legal obligations of suppliers, 56
Legal performance implications of recalls, 19, 91
  civil, 22
  contractual, 22
  criminal, 22
  regulatory, 22
Legal risks, 56
  consumer products, 122
Litigation penalties, 56
Logistical support, 58
Long-term implications, 146
Long-term sustainability in light of the recall, 63
Low risk recall, 98

M

Management information system, 96
Management summary, 145–151
Mandated product recall, 12
Manufacturer notification by suppliers, 56
Marketing expertise product recall task force, 80
Mattel toy 2007 recall, 5–6, 101
Media, 60–63
  common mistake, 62
  dual edged impact, 60
  golden 24 hours rule, 61
  intermediaries, 60
  stonewalling backfire, 62
  trustful relationship, 63

Minimizing Unpleasant Message effect (MUM effect), 56–57
Mislabeled Vanilla Florentine cookies 2024, 59, 107
Mock exercises, 77
Mock recall exercises, 78, 83–85
   continuous enhancement, 85
   implementation and assessment, 83
   scenario development, 83
   stakeholder involvement, 83
Model Declaratory Proceedings, 24, 31
Monitoring of resale platforms, 53
Musterfeststellungsklage, 24, 31

N

Negative overreaction by investors, 35
Non-financial performance implications of recalls, 19, 29–33, 91
   brand hate, 29
   customer disappointment, 29
   customer satisfaction, 29
Number of product recalls, 2

O

Objectives in post-recall phase, 105
Opinion leaders, 60
Opportunity effect, 30
Optimal advertising strategy, 37
Optimal pricing strategy, 37
Overconforming behavior, 32
Overseeing recall process, 54
Owner notification letter, 46

P

Partial remedy, 29
Peloton treadmill 2023 recall, 54
Pepsi's fake product-harm crisis 1993, 92
Performance implications of recalls, 17–37
   financial, 19, 34–37
   legal, 19, 21
   long-term, 19
   non-financial, 19, 29–33
   short-term, 19
Performance recovery in the post-recall phase, 106–108
Philips 2021 recall, 34
Planning, 76–87
Post-recall phase, 70, 105–112
   advertising, 106
   advertising effectiveness, 106
   innovation, 111
   key strategies, 106
   learning, 108–112
   objectives, 105
   performance recovery, 106–108
   price sensitivity, 106
   prices, 106
   safety and learning culture, 110
Precautionary recall, 98
Pre-recall phase, 70
   cross-departmental product recall task force, 78–81
   general product recall guidelines, 81–82
   mock recall exercises, 83–85
   product tracing, safety, and quality assurance, 86–87
   recall training and education program, 82–83

160 Index

Price sensitivity in the post-recall phase, 106
Prices in the post-recall phase, 106
Priority of customers and distributors, 70
Proactive management, 64, 146
Proactive recall management, 35
Problem identification, 89–91
    alpha testing, 90
    beta testing, 89
    delta testing, 90
    external sources, 89
    gamma testing, 89
    internal sources, 89
    quality control, 90
    social media monitoring, 89
    third party test results, 89
Product-harm crisis, 14, 146
Product management cycle, 148
    adaptation to business model and industry, 148
Product recall
    brand damage, 51
    characteristics, 11
    customer-level, 14
    definition, 13, 14
    distribution-level, 15
    involuntary, 12
    mandated, 12
    performance implications, 17–37
    reasons, 2
    voluntary, 12
Product recall management, 146
Product recall management cycle, 69–112
    planning, 76–87
    post-recall phase, 70, 105–112
    pre-recall phase, 70

    recall phase, 70, 87–105
    recall readiness, 76–87
Product registration, 120
Product reliability
    spillover effect, 137, 140
Product removal
    types, 13
Product safety certification, 82
Product safety laws and regulations, 11
Product tampering, 12
Product traceability
    consumer products, 119
    food products, 125
Product tracing, safety, and quality assurance, 78, 86–87
    continuous improvement, 86
    protocols, 86
    regulatory compliance, 86
    supply chain transparency, 86
Product tracking by wholesalers and retailers, 50
Product withdrawal, 13
Promotions after a recall, 35
Public interest, 60
Public policymakers, 53–56

Q

Quality control, 90

R

Reasons for product recalls, 2
Recall advertisement, 100
Recall alert, 44, 45
Recall announcement, 96
    relevant information, 97

Index

Recall completion speed, 104
Recall compliance rate, 103
Recall effectiveness, 103
  automotive products, 130
  recall completion speed, 104
  recall compliance rate, 103
  vehicle products, 130
Recall environment, 34
Recall execution and
    monitoring, 103–104
  implementing remedies, 103
  isolating returned items, 103
  recall completion speed, 104
  recall compliance rate, 103
  recall effectiveness, 103
Recall intensive industries, 35
Recall management
  advertising, 35
  conforming behavior, 32
  customer-centric perspective, 70
  customer expectations, 32
  emotional aspect of customer
      concerns, 71
  hotline for direct customer
      feedback, 36
  optimal advertising strategy, 37
  optimal pricing strategy, 37
  overconforming behavior, 32
  planning, 76–87
  post-recall advertising, 35
  post-recall phase, 70, 105–112
  post-recall promotions, 35
  pre-recall phase, 70
  product recall management
      cycle, 69–112
  proactive, 35
  recall phase, 70, 87–105
  recall readiness, 69, 76–87

reversed marketing strategy, 69
timing of advertising spending,
    37
tracking recall success, 35
underconforming behavior, 32
Recall notification, 44
Recall phase, 70, 87–105
  activities, 88–89
  communication with relevant
      stakeholders, 97–103
  decision on recall, 91–94
  documentation and
      reporting, 104–105
  problem identification, 89–91
  recall execution and
      monitoring, 103–104
  recall plan creation, 94–97
  risk assessment, 91
Recall plan creation, 94–97
  communication strategy, 96
  how-to handbook, 96
  industry regulations, 94
  management information
      system, 96
  recall announcement, 96
  remedy, 95
  simplicity of recall process, 95
  targets, 95
  traceability of recalled
      products, 96
Recall process, 87–105
Recall readiness, 69, 76–87, 147
  components, 78
  cross-departmental product recall
      task force, 78–81
  general product recall guidelines,
      78, 81–82
  mock recall exercises, 78, 83–85

162   Index

Recall readiness (*cont.*)
  product tracing, safety, and
    quality assurance, 78, 86–87
  recall training and education
    program, 78, 82–83
Recall readiness workshops, 83
Recall reasons
  automotive products, 128
  consumer products, 121
  food products, 123
  vehicle products, 128
Recall strategy
  spillover effect, 137, 140
Recall training and education
    program, 78, 82–83
  best practices, 82
  communication guidelines, 82
  protocols for reporting, 82
  recall readiness workshops, 83
  roles and duties, 82
Recommended action, 44
Refund processing, 51
Regulators, 53–56
  approval, 54
  collaboration, 55
  enforcing legal compliance, 54
  escalating efforts, 54
  fostering communication among
    stakeholder, 54
  overseeing recall process, 54
  penalties, 56
  remediation efforts, 55
  reporting requirements, 55
  transparency, 55
Regulatory compliance, 63
Regulatory landscape, 150
  consumer products, 122
Regulatory liability, 22

Regulatory penalties, 56
Relevant information in recall
    announcements, 97
Remediation efforts, 55
Remedy, 29, 95
  automotive products, 128
  consumer products, 118
  food products, 123
  full, 29
  partial, 29
  vehicle products, 128
Reporting requirements, 55
Reputation, 32, 146
Reputation and trust damage, 34
Resale platforms, 52
  continued sell of recalled
    items, 52
  eBay, 52
  engagement, 53
  Etsy, 52
  Facebook, 52
  monitoring, 53
Retailers, 50–53
  assistance, 50
  batch analysis, 58
  contractual obligations, 56
  coordination, 50
  early detection of product
    issues, 50
  ineffective communication, 51
  legal obligations, 56
  logistical support, 58
  missing preparation, 51
  notification of manufacturers, 56
  planning and execution of
    recalls, 58
  product tracking, 50
  refund processing, 51

root cause analysis, 58
tracking components, 58
training and support, 50
trustful relationship with manufacturer, 59
Return instructions, 51
Return process, 51
Reversed marketing strategy, 69
Risk assessment, 91
defect rate, 91
failure rate, 91
financial outcomes, 91
legal liability, 91
market coverage, 91
non-financial outcomes, 91
probability of harm, 91
type of hazard, 91
Risk aversion of investors, 35
Root cause analysis, 58

S

Safety and learning culture, 110
Safety message, 51
Sales effects, 35
Samsung Galaxy Note 7 2016 recall, 1, 51, 98
Sanlu infant formula 2008 recall, 1, 2
Secondary impact recall, 98
Short-term implications, 146
Simplicity of recall process, 95
Social media, 60
Social media firestorm, 61
Social media monitoring, 89
Social media strategy, 98
Space Shuttle Challenger 1986 disaster, 57

Spillover effect, 135–143
advertising of competitor, 138
branding strategy, 137
category effects, 138
competitor association, 137
competitor similarity, 137
country of origin, 137, 139
denial strategy, 140
guilty by association-effect, 136, 140
key factors, 141
passive recall, 140
prices of competitor, 138
proactive recall, 98, 140
product reliability, 137, 140
recall strategy, 137, 140
spillover on B2B customers, 141–143
spillover on competitors, 137–141
spillover on same-company products, 136–137
Spillover on B2B customers, 141–143
Spillover on competitors, 137–141
Spillover on same-company products, 136–137
Spokesperson during recall, 100
Stakeholder groups, 43–65
customers, 44–49
distributors, 50–53
financial analysts, 63–65
investors, 63–65
journalists, 60–63
media, 60–63
priority of customers and distributors, 70
public policymakers, 53–56

Stakeholder groups (cont.)
  regulators, 53–56
  retailers, 50–53
  suppliers, 56–59
  supportive roles, 70
  wholesalers, 50–53
Standardized procedures, 81
Stock recovery, 12
Stonewalling backfire, 62
Suppliers, 56–59
Supply chain
  consumer products, 119
Supportive roles of stakeholder groups, 70

T

Takata Corp airbag 2013 recall, 2, 20, 127
Targets for recall plan creation, 95
Technological advancements, 148
Third party test results, 89
Timing of advertising spending, 37
Top10 key takeaways, 145–151
Traceability of recalled products, 96
Tracking components, 58
Tracking recall success, 35
Training and support of wholesalers and retailers, 50
Training programs, 76
Transparency, 64
Transparency in the supply chain, 57
Transparency with regulators, 55

Trustful relationship between supplier and manufacturer, 59
Trustful relationship with media, 63
Types of product removals, 13

U

Underconforming behavior, 32
Unprepared retailers, 51
Use of media during recall, 103

V

Vehicle products, 126–131
  recall effectiveness, 130
  recall reasons, 128
  remedy, 128
Volkswagen's Dieselgate, 24–25, 31, 106, 139
Voluntary product recall, 12

W

Westland/Hallmark beef 2008 recall, 1
Wholesalers, 50–53
  assistance, 50
  coordination, 50
  early detection of product issues, 50
  product tracking, 50
  training and support, 50
Wipe-out effect, 30

SPRINGER NATURE

GPSR Compliance

The European Union's (EU) General Product Safety Regulation (GPSR) is a set of rules that requires consumer products to be safe and our obligations to ensure this.

If you have any concerns about our products, you can contact us on ProductSafety@springernature.com

In case Publisher is established outside the EU, the EU authorized representative is:

Springer Nature Customer Service Center GmbH
Europaplatz 3
69115 Heidelberg, Germany

The manufacturer's authorised representative in the EU is Springer Nature Customer Service Centre GmbH, Europaplatz 3, 69115 Heidelberg, Germany. If you have any concerns regarding our products, please contact ProductSafety@springernature.com

Printed and bound by CPI Group (UK) Ltd, Croydon, CR0 4YY

23/03/2026

02076399-0001